# Contents

KU-216-632

*"Don't do unto others as you would they would do unto you because they're different and they won't like it!"*

GEORGE BERNARD SHAW

# Foreword

The Commission for Racial Equality was established by Parliament to work for the elimination of racial discrimination and the promotion of equality of opportunity and good race relations. However, the quest for racial equality and justice is one which must involve all public agencies in British society, and the Commission seeks to work with all such bodies in order to achieve the objectives of race relations legislation.

The Commission is, therefore, extremely pleased to welcome the initiative taken by the West Midlands County Probation and After-Care Service in producing this comprehensive report on 'Probation and After-Care in a Multi-Racial Society' which highlights an urgent need to review policies. Although the report deals with the position in one multi-racial metropolitan county, the Commission believes that there is much in the contents, conclusions and recommendations which should commend them to probation services throughout Britain.

This is the first report to be published on probation and racial equality and is the result of considerable work since the Home Office advised the Probation Services in 1976 of the need to promote a professional approach to the racial dimensions of it's task. As such it is very welcome. It stands alongside a parallel report on 'Multi-Racial Britain – The Social Services Response', which the Commission published with the Association of Directors of Social Services in 1978.

The major concern and priority of the Commission is the needs of children and young people in our society. We published our policy report on 'Youth in Multi-Racial Society' in 1980, which we subtitled 'The Fire Next Time'. The highest proportion of black clients in contact with the probation service are juveniles and young persons, and much of the work undertaken with the young black offender is during or following custodial sentences.

The reasons why a high proportion of young blacks come before the courts are many and various. Not least among these is the considerably greater difficulty they have in finding employment than their comparable white peers, and the anger they feel as a response to the prejudice and discrimination they experience during their formative years.

The future of multi-racial society in Britain rests in large part on the treatment experienced by the younger generation. The bridges created to enable young blacks who are in trouble with authority to come back into society without bitterness, and to make their contribution to the country's future, are crucial. The role of the Probation Service in this process is of the greatest importance.

The Commission would make the recommendations listed on the next page to the Probation Service and to the Home Office.

**David Lane**
*Chairman*
Commission for Racial Equality

# CRE RECOMMENDATIONS

The Commission recommends that the *Probation and After-Care Services* should:

1. Undertake surveys to discover the extent, location and nature of their work with minority ethnic groups, resulting from both court orders and custodial sentences.

2. Initiate a separate study of the work undertaken at the *Social Enquiry Report* stage.

3. Continue to collect up to date and accurate statistics concerning the position of racial minorities as suggested by the Home Office Advisory Committee on Race Relations Research in 1975.

4. Develop new professional approaches in dealing with clients from ethnic minority groups as suggested in Home Office Circular 113/1977.

5. Encourage and support public education about the Probation and After-Care Services among ethnic minority communities.

6. Enter into partnership with the ethnic minority communities so that the Service builds on their caring strengths and networks.

7. Encourage the recruitment of more ethnic minority Probation Staff, as well as black volunteers, ancillary workers and interpreters.

8. Set up schemes and projects to support and assist young black offenders, that take into account the experience and opportunities of ethnic minority people in British society.

9. Set up more Intermediate Treatment Schemes for young offenders.

10. Provide regular training for all staff about the needs of ethnic minorities and their position in British society. Staff need to be en-

couraged to expand their experiences and methods to provide a more relevant and sensitive service.

11. Make policy statements to ensure that they do not subscribe to any actions or practices which may be discriminating and adversely affect minority ethnic groups.

The Commission recommend that the *Home Office* should:

1. Undertake a study of the effect of sentencing practices and procedures on ethnic minorities, particularly on young blacks.

# 1.   Introduction

1.1   This document presents information and opinions given by staff at all levels of the West Midlands County Probation and After-Care Service in relation to the work of the Service with ethnic minority groups and, in particular, with black people in the West Midlands County.

1.2   It identifies real concern about the position of black people in society, focusing particularly upon those who come into contact with the Probation Service as a result of involvement with the legal and penal systems. Issues are raised which can be affected by immediate changes in policy and practice and others which require further exploration before effective action can be taken.

1.3   There is no intention to interpret the statistical information in the report at this stage and those who do so run the risk of misinterpreting complex issues, as many other factors beyond the bounds of this report would also need to be considered. This survey exposes areas which clearly call for further investigation, not only by the Probation and After-Care Service but by others concerned with the equality of justice for offenders.

1.4   It is recognised there may be those who will attempt to use the information presented to discredit black people; we consider the data does not do that, but that factor alone often precludes publication of this type of material and so facts concerning the treatment of black people in our community are withheld, and do not become open to investigation.

1.5   West Midlands County Probation and After-Care Service believes that it has both the right and responsibility to address itself to the social concerns of the black community and that as part of the legal and penal systems it cannot evaluate its work effectively in isolation from society. The report can be seen as an attempt to draw a baseline in a previously uncharted area, from which future progress (or decline) can be measured.

1.6   In offering this domestic document to a wider readership it is hoped that it will encourage others to identify their responsibilities and explore their attitudes towards the black members of our community, thus assisting the Probation Service in its efforts to evaluate its contribution within society.

**Michael Day O.B.E.**
*Chief Probation Officer*
West Midlands County Probation and After-Care Service

# 2. The Probation and After-Care Service

2.1   The Probation and After-Care Service is a national organisation divided for administrative purposes into 56 autonomous Probation and After-Care Areas.

2.2   The Home Secretary is responsible to Parliament for the efficiency of the service, to ensure proper use of public funds and that the Service is fulfilling the demands placed upon it by statute.

2.3   Probation Officers are employed neither by Central nor Local Government, but by Probation and After-Care Committees, whose main responsibilities are the organisation and administration of the Area Service. They are charged with the provision of a Service which encompasses a wide range of tasks considered essential to the well-being of the community, namely:

(a) the supervision of offenders at the order of the criminal courts;
(b) the supervision of offenders released from custody;
(c) the supervision of children at the order of the civil courts;
(d) the provision of social inquiry reports for the criminal courts;
(e) the provision of welfare reports for the civil courts;
(f) the provision of hostels, day centres, accommodation and other facilities for offenders;
(g) the provision of facilities for community service;
(h) the provision of an internal social work service for the prisons and other penal establishments.[1]

2.4   The aim of the service is:

"To contribute to the better personal and social functioning of individuals to whom the Service has responsibilities: to provide acceptable alternatives to custodial sentences within the criminal justice system, to contribute to the quality of the work of the courts and to contribute to the well-being of

---

[1]Report of the Working Party on Management Structure in the Probation and After-Care Service – published 1980.

the community and particularly to the containment and reduction of criminal behaviour".[1]

**West Midlands County Probation and After-Care Service**

2.5    The West Midlands County Probation and After-Care Service (WMCPACS) is the second largest Service in the country serving a population of 2,696,000, distributed across 347 square miles. Birmingham alone contains an estimated 1,033,900 people.[2]

There are 25 Probation Offices from which 372 officers operate.

Office locations are shown in Map 1.

Officers are deployed as listed in Appendix 2. Table 1. The West Midlands County is divided into 8 operational Probation Sub-Areas. Map 1.

Officers are supported by administrative and clerical staff, ancillary workers, volunteers and other personnel.

2.6    All categories of client contact (as listed a–h) include work with people of diverse racial and cultural backgrounds. It is in relation to the tasks and aims of the Probation Service, that WMCPACS seeks to address itself to its legal and moral responsibilities in regard to the provision and delivery of its service to members of all ethnic minority groups, but to black people[3] in particular.

2.7    No regular forum exists for the exchange of information and development of work with ethnic minorities within the Probation Service nationally. At the present time it is for the individual County Services to make their own links with Probation Services in other parts of the country. It is therefore likely that there has been an amount of duplication of work and little circulation of data or discussion within the Service of developments in this area of work.

**Ethnic Minorities and the Probation Service**

2.8    The dimension of need related to the ethnic minority groups in general and the black communities in particular are important considerations for the Probation Officer.

---

[1]Defined by West Yorkshire PACS in the above report.
[2]Office of population cencuses and surveys – OPCS monitor – ref. PP1 80/2 – mid-1979 population estimates. Issue 24.6.1980.
[3]Definition of terms used – Appendix 5.

12

### (a) The relative newness of the black communities

2.9      The Probation Officer is a servant of both Government and the community. As an agent of the court he is viewed as part of the legal and penal system but is also a trained social worker concerned with assisting the functioning of an individual within society. This is a difficult dual role to establish, even more so when engaging with people who:

     (i) may not have heard of the Probation Service,
     (ii) may apply a different cultural connotation to the role of a 'social worker'.

2.10      The social welfare system in Britain is complex and confusing, members of ethnic minorities are even less likely to know or understand the Probation Service, how it works and how to approach it for relevant assistance than other citizens. They may believe that their traditions and cultures would not be respected by the service, or merely that communication would be difficult. The Probation Officer should work to improve the understanding of the service by the public, and especially by ethnic groups. The Probation Officer can often work more successfully with ethnic minorities if he works through the local support networks which stem from kin and religious institutions.

### (b) Cultural differences

2.11      Within a multi-racial community there is a wide variety of languages, cultures and religions which over centuries of time have formed the basis for the development of different life-styles. Attitudes, beliefs, expectations, behaviour and ways of ordering and structuring families, communities and individual relationships have developed which differ, often substantially from the western systems.

2.12      The growth in Britain's multi-cultural community has led to varieties of language, religions and cultures which have existed in Britain for many years gaining more prominence and visibility. Therefore it is important that probation staff do not apply western values where they are not appropriate whether in education or counselling. If Probation Services wish to provide their services effectively to ethnic groups they will need to review the adaptability of their services; staff will need additional training and the support of interpreters if they are to provide a satisfactory service both to clients and the courts.

### (c) Prejudice and discrimination

2.13      "Racial prejudice and the resulting discrimination are factors which make ethnic minorities more exposed and more vulnerable. This may increase their need for support from public services and must be taken into account as a very real factor by those providing services to them."[1]

2.14 Racism is the effect of prejudice combined with the opportunity or power to affect someone negatively by discriminating against them. Probation Officers, Magistrates, Prison Officers, Social Workers, Teachers and the Police have many more powers than the private citizen and thus far greater opportunities to discriminate both directly and indirectly. They therefore have greater responsibilities to use their powers to combat discrimination than the private citizen.

2.15 Jerome Cohen[2] writes of the powerful and pervasive influence which race exerts on the delivery of a professional service, and of the quiet unintentional dissuasive influences operating even when overt discrimination is a rarity.

2.16 There are, therefore, two areas to be taken into account constantly:

(a) the prejudice and discrimination suffered by ethnic minorities
(b) attitudes which affect the provision of service to ethnic minorities.

[1]Multi-Racial Britain: The Social Services Response. ADSS and CRE Report.
[2]'Race as a Factor in Social Work Practice.' – Jerome Cohen.

# 3. Review of Policy and Practice

3.1    In early 1976, the Probation and After-Care Department and Race Relations Adviser at the Home Office reviewed the extent to which the Service was aware of the special considerations affecting its work with 'clients from ethnic minority groups' and the steps that might be taken to increase this awareness.

3.2    An exploratory meeting between the Probation and After-Care Department, and the Race Relations Adviser at the Home Office and representatives from five probation areas and two regional staff development offices was held at the Home Office in April, 1976, as a result of which it was decided that a workshop organised at national level for senior members of the service would be a desirable first step. In the event, two seminars, each extending over four days and with similar programmes, were held in London in October and November, 1976. The first of these was attended by senior representatives of the Metropolitan Counties and the second by members of other areas which were thought to have 'a significant ethnic minority population.'

3.3    The following conclusions were reached:

(a) There was a need for the Service generally to promote a professional approach to the racial dimensions of its task and that, in some areas, this represented an urgent priority.
(b) It was agreed a wider understanding of the cultural background of the ethnic groups was essential to the development of a greater awareness of the racial dimensions and, thereby, to a more sensitive and effective relationship with individual clients.
(c) The need for such knowledge should be reflected in staff development programmes.
(d) Basic information about race relations legislation was identified as a further requirement.
(e) It was recognised that further liaison with local ethnic groups and other agencies with experience of particular areas in developing new profes-

sional approaches in dealing with clients from ethnic minority groups could be beneficial to the Probation Service.[1]

3.4  All Probation and After-Care Committees were invited to examine the particular problems and needs of their own areas in this context and develop training courses as appropriate for their staffs.

3.5  It was suggested that in 'each area with a significant ethnic minority population', one officer should be appointed to act as a point for reference on race relations matters.

3.6  It was envisaged the role of such officers would be:

(a) to promote liaison with local organisations whose activities are relevant to the work of the service;
(b) to stimulate the organisation of any arrangements for training which might be thought appropriate for each area;
(c) to exchange information with other probation areas and Regional Staff Development Officers;
(d) To liaise with the Probation and After-Care Department on development in race relations matters of regional or national interest.

3.7  It was not intended that the organisation of experience in race relations matters should be regarded as a specialism, experience being seen as relevant to staff at all levels.

3.8  In November 1979 the Race Relations Advisor to the Home Office commented that following the meetings between herself and Senior management of the Probation Service in 1977, some Probation Services became more active than others but that they were few in number and the overall approach to cultural development in social work in the Probation Service has been one of ambivalence.

'The Service in general – possibly without realising it – has neglected this area of work, overlooking group inter-action in the community because of the traditional focus of one-to-one case work.'

**The Response of the West Midlands**

3.9  The West Midlands County Probation and After-Care Service responded initially by designating an Assistant Chief Probation Officer as Ethnic Liaison Officer for the County in addition to administrative responsibilities

---

[1] H.O. Circular. 113/1977 – PACS: Ethnic Minorities.

for his own area. This officer left the service and another Assistant Chief Probation Officer then undertook this responsibility. Similar responses had occurred in other Counties with officers of different grades undertaking this additional new role.

3.10 In the West Midlands, the County with the second highest composition of different ethnic groups in the country, it became clear that the cultural dimension was an area of work which was in need of development and exploration in which a central and collective approach would be more realistic.

3.11 Financial resources were available for the appointment of one officer to address himself/herself full time to the expansion of work in this field, and a Working Party was convened, consisting of two Assistant Chief Probation Officers and representatives from each sub-area, to consider the viability of such an appointment. Proposals were made to management, that one full time worker at Senior Probation Officer grade should be appointed, to operate centrally, and a framework of the responsibilities of such post was outlined.

3.12 The proposed job specification of the Ethnic Adviser was:

(1) To be a focal point of information about ethnic minorities to the County Probation Service. Amongst other things, this will involve obtaining and compiling information about ethnic groups, about relevant resources in the area (including interpreters) and about methods of working with ethnic minorities.
(2) In conjunction with the Training Section of the County Service, to promote appropriate training opportunities for officers in the County Service and also possibly to contribute to local CQSW training courses.
(3) To maintain appropriate links with other agencies within the County, including Police, Community Relations Councils and other ethnic minority specialists. To represent the County in appropriate local and national forums and to maintain suitable links with other Probation Areas.
(4) To advise the Chief Probation Officer in delicate situations which arise within the County Service, including cases of discrimination.
(5) To advise the County Management Team on appropriate policies, resource requirements and difficulties relating to ethnic minorities.

3.13 The recommendations of the Working Party were accepted by management and on 1st August, 1979, a Senior Probation Officer was appointed to work full time in this field with the title of, 'County Adviser to West Midlands Probation and After-Care Service on Ethnic Minorities'. By making this appointment, management made clear the importance placed on this dimension of work in the West Midlands Probation Service. Despite the use of the term 'Ethnic Minorities' in the title, it was clearly seen that the primary focus of the post was in the work of the Service in relation to black people.

**An Internal Review of Services to Ethnic Minorities**

3.14   During the 3 months (September-December 1979) following appointment, the Adviser visited every Probation Office in the County, Specialist Units, Hostels, HM Prison Winson Green, and talked with Project Organisers. Discussion took place with staff at all levels in a variety of ways, by joining in regular Team Meetings, by attending Joint Team Meetings for discussion in larger groups, by convening special meetings for debate on this subject and some individual officers gave personal opinions in private interviews. Over three hundred staff took part.

3.15   The aims of this communication exercise were as follows:

(1) To introduce the post of Ethnic Adviser as a County resource.
(2) To encourage the free expression of attitudes of Officers towards engaging in work in this field.
(3) To discover the practical needs of Officers to enable effective Service delivery.
(4) To stimulate the exchange of ideas and information both within the County Service and nationally.
(5) To evaluate current policy and practice with a view to forward planning and action.

3.16   The following sections present information and opinion gathered during the course of the internal review.

**Social and Professional Issues**

3.17   There are problems evident which social work alone cannot hope to eradicate or even alleviate, as many spring from the structural problems of society. These require social and economic changes. Some problems arise from disadvantages suffered by black people which require special measures by the various services. Others arise from prejudice and discrimination which often require special measures also and sufficient emphasis by all concerned on improving race relations.

3.18   Social and moral conscience press some officers towards the wider issues of social policy. They feel strongly that one way of contributing towards the well being of the community – and in particular certain groups of its disadvantaged members – is to seek to influence the policy makers. Equally there are officers who oppose the activities of colleagues who are thought to be entering into a political arena and their motives for doing so are questioned.

3.19   Officers in close contact with black people have repeatedly raised a number of issues questioning how society's problems can be tackled effectively by working at an individual level. Many officers advocate corporate action and close involvement with other agencies and systems. The focus of their concern lies in the following areas:

(1) The underlying sense of injustice which is felt by many (some would say 'most') black people of their reception and treatment by a 'white' society.
(2) The specific feelings of injustice expressed towards the law enforcement agencies and the legal and penal system.
(3) The prejudice and discrimination evident in every facet of life, often commencing during early formative years and frequently preventing social and economic progress, frustrating aspirations and ambitions.
(4) The education system within which black people often fail to reach their potential leaving under-educated and under-skilled.
(5) The comparatively high unemployment rate amongst the young black population.
(6) The acute difficulties experienced by the young black male seeking independent accommodation.
(7) Emotional conflict which is often related to the shock of transition from one culture to another and the search for a cultural identity.
(8) The alienation of a small, but significant number of black youth from 'white' society.

3.20   Officers comment that the group most seriously affected over-all are Afro/Caribbean people, especially *young* blacks.

3.21   Many of these issues are considered in more detail in 'The Fire Next Time'[1] where it is pointed out that despite the recommendations by the Hunt Committee in 1967 and the warning that '. . . if England is not to be the scene of race riots . . . the time for action is now . . .'[2] Lamentably little has been done, nor have services adequately modified their practices to meet the changing needs of a multi-racial society.

3.22   Officers seeking to draw attention to these issues and bring about changes have met with some resistance and criticism but have also gained support and certain action has been taken as a result of their initiatives. There is strong support for the opinion that conventional case-work methods are proving inadequate, particularly in respect of the service offered to black people.

3.23   Opposing opinion advocates a policy of inaction and containment. There are officers who view the rise of such movements as Rastafarianism as a phase in black youth seeking a common identity comparable to white youth culture such as Skin Heads, Hells Angels and Punk Rockers.

3.24   There are also views expressed that focus upon the black ethnic groups is an admission of a separatist approach which mitigates against a policy of integration. However, others point out that until such problems as the black people are experiencing within society are recognised and acted upon by those who *are* in a position to instigate changes, however slow this process may be, there will be no possibility of harmonious long term co-existence within society.

3.25   There is, therefore, no one collective voice within the Service, but as many voices with differing views as there are within society. But it is the voice of change which is making itself heard as the need of the black people continues to increase.

3.26   A Senior Probation Officer who has been trying to raise interest amongst individuals in the policy and practice within their own agencies writes:

3.27   'What is required is that active and unintentional discrimination is eradicated by vigilant monitoring of services offered. Collusion with racist policies must cease and commitment to undertake good social work in a multi-racial context must be taken at a personal level and at the levels of management and policy making. That we are dealing in a

---

[1]Youth in Multi-Racial Society – 'The Fire Next Time' CRE publication.
[2]'Immigrants and the Youth Service' – Report of the Committee of the Youth

political and sensitive arena is self-evident. It must, however, be recognised that inaction is equally a political position.'[1]

3.28 Government policy affects the everyday lives of members of society and important issues arise such as the recent changes in the Immigration Rules which affect some sections of the community more than others. The Probation Officer needs to be aware of the views of the community on political decisions and as an individual will speak and act in accordance with his own conscience in the light of his own perceptions of the situation.

3.29 In response to the Government's White Paper published on 14 November 1979 entitled 'Proposals for Revision of the Immigration Rules'. 10 Probation Officers, acting collectively, prepared a statement detailing their concern in relation to certain of the proposals which it was thought selectively and directly discriminated against black people. After consultation of the issues involved certain correspondence ensued between the Chief Probation Officer and the Home Secretary as a result.

3.30 Management therefore need to be kept well informed by officers who are in close contact with all sections of the community, in order to offer support when it is possible and appropriate and in order to plan its own policies in the light of the social situation within the community.

**The Probation Service and Black People in the Community**

3.31 During the compilation of this report it became increasingly clear that the image of the Probation Service in the community needs attention, particularly in relation to the black communities who need to be enabled to make better use of the services offered. The comment by a Coventry CRC Officer that Asians believe it is not a Service for *them* makes one ask 'why not?'

3.32 The Probation Service needs to publicise its activities and functions especially to ethnic minorities. The message that the Probation Service is available to all races and cultures needs to be communicated by all staff, as it appears to be currently in question.

3.33 Suggestions of ways in which the Probation Service could help black people to understand, use or join the Probation Service could include:

(a) personal contact with black leaders, visits to and talks at religious centres, community centres, clubs, black organisations, schools etc.

---

[1]P. Whitehouse S.P.O. Birmingham North. Unpublished paper on 'Racial Discrimination'.

(b) articles in the black press, particularly in regard to Probation Orders, publicising Community Service as an alternative to Prison, advertisement of vacancies for professional, administrative, secretarial and clerical staff and information relating to the recruitment and use of voluntary associates.

(c) identifying information centres used by black people, such as their local shops, law centres, resource centres, etc, and ensuring that information regarding our function is understood and available.

(d) providing leaflets in various languages outlining the function of the Probation Service with addresses of local offices available for general distribution.

(e) publicity available in greater detail, particularly for use by court duty officers and solicitors, outlining the purpose of Social Enquiry reports and the type of information that would be requested.

3.34    The involvement of black communities in the review of existing practices is crucial to the development of effective services. Therefore, in undertaking any further research in this area, it is vital that close links are developed with the local black communities in order that they may contribute. Such involvement may well provide a platform for people to express views on current service delivery, and areas which need to be considered. Working together with community groups should help to expand cultural understanding and stimulate thinking about methods and approaches.

3.35    The information which Probation Officers gather about their areas needs to be collated and shared. The benefits of knowing the composition of the ethnic minority communities, their structure and their leaders is of inestimable value when assessing a member of that community and his functioning within it and within society. Often a community view is available of the family; their respectability, status and standing within the community which are not easy matters to assess and which give an additional base from which to work.[1] It is strongly recommended that officers working in multi-cultural areas should learn all they can about their patch and link closely with the networks and support systems which sustain the communities living there. This will help them to make individual relationships and avoid making such basic mistakes as referring to a Sikh temple as a 'Mosque'. It is not difficult to get to know ethnic communities. The Asian population especially tend to live in clearly definable communities differentiated by religion and background. To work with a community is the best way to learn how to serve it.

---

[1]There are different cultural perceptions of 'confidentiality' which would need to be explored in relation to individual situations.

### 'Self-help' groups in the Community

3.36 The Funding Register for ethnic minority self-help groups compiled by the Home Office Research Unit is a 500 page document detailing the Home Office and Commission for Racial Equality initiatives in channeling help to ethnic minority communities, many of which have been particularly directed towards helping the alienated youth through self-help groups. The Register includes as many groups run by ethnic minorities as it has been possible to identify but it includes the fullest information on West Indian, African, Bengali, Pakistani and Indian organisations.

3.37 The term 'self-help' is defined as one in which members of a group are engaged in helping themselves as individuals rather than looking for substitute professional support. The register outlines a distinction between groups formed to provide mutual benefit for all members (where each person joins primarily for his or her own self-help) and groups formed to provide support for certain individual members in trouble (where unpaid fellow members are used as sources of aid instead of paid professionals).

3.38 The register states in the Introduction:

'The growth in the number of ethnic minority self-help groups in Britain has been based upon the need to restore and continue a pride in cultural, racial or regional identity to counteract the demoralising practical and psychological effects of failure and discrimination, and to re-establish a sense of community among minorities suffering from differing degrees of disadvantage'. Contact with the groups may provide resources and an alternative approach to helping individuals by a supportive linking process.

# 4. Local Information, Issues and Responses

4.1 Within the West Midlands County, as other counties, there are wide variations of settlement pattern and social needs. Appendix 3 analyses the social and economic conditions of the ethnic minorities in the West Midlands. In this chapter, we seek to relate some of the statistics to local settings, highlighting some of the ways in which local issues give rise to initiatives and responses at the local level. The chapter is divided into discussion of each of the probation sub areas in the West Midlands.

### Wolverhampton (Probation Sub Area A)

| Category of Supervision | Total on area caseloads | No. & % of ethnic minorities on caseload | |
|---|---|---|---|
| Probation | 221 | 36 | (16.3%) |
| C & YP Supervision | 102 | 35 | (34.3%) |
| Suspended Sentence Supn. | 24 | 2 | (8.3%) |
| Money Payment Supn. | — | — | — |
| Detention Centre Licence | 48 | 22 | (45.8%) |
| Borstal Licence | 45 | 7 | (15.5%) |
| Prison Licence | 23 | 4 | (17.4%) |
| Parole | 23 | 10 | (43.5%) |
| Voluntary After Care | 6 | 3 | (50.0%) |
| Pre-release | 203 | 43 | (21.2%) |
| Matrimonial & Wardship | 45 | 3 | (6.7%) |
| Kindred Social Work | 8 | — | — |
| **TOTAL** | **748** | **165** | **(22.3%)** |

4.2 The composition of the ethnic groups in Wolverhampton and their present position as members of the local community are outlined in the 'Wolverhampton Structure Plan' as follows:

4.3 "In 1971, 8.6% of the population of Wolverhampton was of new Commonwealth origin, predominantly Asian but with a substantial number of West Indians. This percentage has increased with a concentration of immigrants in the priority area and the importance of effective action in this field cannot be overstressed. The Inner Area Programme is concerned above all with improving the quality of life. There is undoubtedly a growing feeling of isolation, not only amongst the immigrant community, but also amongst long term residents who find their traditional community disappearing. The sense of isolation is developing into alienation, particularly amongst some young West Indians who look, for example, towards Rastafarianism as something with which they can identify that is clearly not part of the white community.

4.4 The different cultural and religious backgrounds of minority groups produce different problems.[1] Within any group of recent immigrants there is a strong desire for cultural identity. This is evident as much among Poles and Ukranians as it is among Asians and West Indians. Where colour is involved however the consciousness of difference is increased.

4.5 Social problems can be summarised as:

(a) Children and youth at risk from a variety of family, cultural and environmental circumstances leading to delinquency, vandalism, truancy, etc;
(b) Isolation, particularly amongst the elderly, both native and immigrant;
(c) Incompatibility between different groups of people living in a densely populated area, particularly the elderly and the young and on occasion, with different cultural and social traditions;
(d) The search for or loss of community and cultural identity;
(e) The poor reputation of certain areas, resulting in further intensification of problems;
(f) The concentrations of people under the most serious stress."

4.6 Wolverhampton is covered by 4 probation field teams. Three teams are based at Wolverhampton and one at Bilston. At the time of this survey reorganisation of the deployment of officers was taking place. The social problems of the area were generally well recognised and some individual officers had been focusing particularly on the needs of the black groups. Between 21 September, 1978, and 20 December, 1979, a Probation Officer experimented in running a group for young Asians who were under supervision, which proved most successful. During the 15 months it was operational, membership totalled 13, average age 16 years. Five orders were discharged as no longer in need of supervision and 2 left the group (one to personal supervision and one made subject to a Care Order). There

---

[1]Differences are apparently equated with 'problems'.

were no re-offenders whilst the group was operational and one re-offender since closure of the group. The group ran with the assistance of a volunteer and student involvement. Activities included outings to cinemas, swimming, orienteering, wrestling (as spectators), visits to youth clubs, one weekend away, and one week spent Youth Hostelling. Financing was by donations from local organisations and a £250 grant from Urban Aid. This group has attracted interest from outside WMCPACS.

4.7 Another officer is taking a M.Phil. Degree at Aston University. He is examining 'Motivational Accounts of Ethnic Minority Offenders of Asian and West Indian Origins'. This will necessitate taking full details of the Wolverhampton office intake of juvenile offenders during 1979, running this information through the computers and looking for patterns of difference between Asian, West Indian and indigenous offender populations. He will also look at their sentencing patterns. As a hypothesis develops this will be tested out by interviewing a sample of offenders.

4.8 There is a wider concern regarding the juvenile offender in Wolverhampton. NACRO is currently undertaking research to provide a juvenile offender profile of the area at the invitation of Social Services Department.

4.9 The initial investigations indicate that in Wolverhampton there is a significantly higher than average chance of a juvenile receiving a custodial sentence. The statistical survey shows that 45.8% of all young people on Detention Centre Licence in Wolverhampton as at 30 November 1979 were black. This is the highest percentage in this category in the county. It is a matter of concern.

4.10 Representatives of Social Services, the Police, the Probation Service and NACRO have joined together to consider initiatives for the development of a Community Centred Programme in response to this situation.

4.11 A NACRO/YOP employment programme taking a high proportion of black clients is based in the Wolverhampton Probation Office.

**Dudley/Warerley (Probation Sub Area B)**

4.12 This area is covered by 6 single teams. Each team is situated on its own geographical patch and therefore serves a definable local community each of which differs substantially. The number of ethnic minorities on caseload at each office gives some indication of the spread of ethnic groups.

Smethwick (65)     Dudley (26)     Oldbury (20)
Brierley Hill (3)     Stourbridge (3)     Halesowen (1)

| Category of Supervision | Total on area caseload | No. & % of ethnic minorities on caseload | |
|---|---|---|---|
| Probation | 343 | 29 | (8.5%) |
| C & YP Supervision | 135 | 11 | (8.2%) |
| Suspended Sentence Supn. | 17 | 2 | (11.8%) |
| Money Payment Supn. | 14 | 2 | (14.3%) |
| Detention Centre Licence | 49 | 5 | (10.2%) |
| Borstal Licence | 29 | 8 | (27.6%) |
| Prison Licence | 15 | 2 | (13.3%) |
| Parole | 24 | 8 | (33.3%) |
| Voluntary After-Care | 38 | 7 | (18.4%) |
| Pre-release | 283 | 18 | (6.4%) |
| Matrimonial & Wardship | 218 | 26 | (11.9%) |
| Kindred social work | 57 | 6 | (10.5%) |
| **TOTAL** | **1222** | **124** | **(10.2%)** |

(a) **Smethwick:**

4.13 The present numbers of Indians under supervision do not reflect the large Sikh community concentrated in this small patch and numbers can fluctuate; sometimes numbers increase following custodial sentences for groups of those involved in affrays.

4.14 There has been a Community approach in involving the use of volunteers from the local community both formally and informally and linking with the Gurdwara (Sikh Temple) (whose Professor is also the Sikh religious adviser for H.M. Prison, Winson Green). One problem has been in finding female volunteers from the Sikh community. Two Sikh volunteers are always engaged in different kinds of voluntary work and are indispensable to this office.

4.15 The office policy has been to allow officers with particular interest in different ethnic groups to pursue their interests by taking the major amount of work evolving from that group. A Probation Officer speaking Asian languages has recently been appointed.

4.16 Officers involved with West Indian clients point towards the urgent problems of accommodation and employment, particularly for the younger age

27

groups. A collective approach has been taken regarding employment through meetings with the Department of Employment.

4.17 An officer is compiling data relating to the nature of offences of all Asians appearing before the court during the last three years and is linking this to sentences received. It is hoped a comparable study of a sample of the indigenous population will be possible.

### (b) Oldbury:

4.18 This is an old area without definable communities and different ethnic groups are scattered across the patch. All officers have black clients on their caseloads. They comment that there is not sufficient ethnic work to build up any depth of experience and it is a continual cultural learning process. Oldbury have linked with Smethwick in the training of volunteers and have access to the Sikh volunteers who live in Smethwick.

### (c) Dudley:

4.19 Dudley officers were the most positive of all office groups in regard to the impact which collective policy locally has had on the situation of the black groups in the Area. They also spoke of local personalities who had taken initiatives in assisting integration.

4.20 The group with the highest representation on caseloads is West Indian with 16 under supervision. Concern had been expressed by a new officer regarding the duplication of problems which were being presented by young unsupported West Indian mothers. The possibility of group advice was being considered. There is a Young Wives' group which is multi-racial.

4.21 Dudley CRC adds another perspective. They give figures as: total population 300,800 – total ethnic minorities 12,750, which are mainly Asians, and 3,500 West Indians. It is suggested that closer monitoring of black people appearing before Dudley court would show clearly whether this large Asian community either have a very low proportion of offenders or whether they do not reach the Probation Service as there are only 4 Asians in contact through custodial sentences and 1 C & Y.P. under supervision.

4.22 CRC confirm the officer's impressions that the extent of racial problems may well be considerably less in this area but add that this does not necessarily mean that there are no problems to consider.

## (d) Brierley Hill, Stourbridge and Halesowen:

4.23 These three teams covering half the area are in roughly the same position in regard to the nature and amount of work with black people. Officers in all 3 offices have given instances of involvement in enquiries needing cultural knowledge and expertise, some of complexity, and some with serious repercussions after decisions had been made in the courts. Such cases obviously make a lasting impression, and officers are aware they may take up extra time and that they also need to consider the use of other resources. There is recognition that use of volunteers/interpreters/advisers and a consultancy service could provide a wider perception of cultural aspects and contribute towards expanding officers' cultural knowledge.

## (e) Area Training

4.24 A series of training afternoons on 'Violence in the Family' included a cultural 'strand', considering family dynamics in the Asian and West Indian Family in conflict. Interest was raised and the formation of a small Area group has been proposed to look at the subject in greater depth.

### Walsall/West Bromwich (Probation Sub Area C)

| Category of Supervision | Total on area caseload | No. & % of ethnic minorities on caseload | |
|---|---|---|---|
| Probation | 241 | 18 | (7.5%) |
| C & Y.P. Supervision | 127 | 6 | (4.7%) |
| Suspended Sentence Supn. | 18 | 1 | (5.6%) |
| Money Payment Supn. | 14 | — | — |
| Detention Centre Licence | 58 | 7 | (12.1%) |
| Borstal Licence | 46 | 8 | (17.4%) |
| Prison Licence | 20 | 1 | (5.0%) |
| Parole | 23 | 1 | (4.3%) |
| Voluntary After-Care | 37 | 1 | (2.7%) |
| Pre-release | 236 | 18 | (7.6%) |
| Matrimonial & Wardship | 140 | 5 | (3.6%) |
| Kindred Social Work | 36 | 1 | (2.8%) |
| **TOTAL** | **996** | **67** | **(6.7%)** |

4.25 The 1971 Census list a New Commonwealth born population of approximately 9,000 in the Walsall County Borough which was smaller than the present Metropolitan Borough. This represented about 1 in 20 of the population. This figure was broken down into ethnic groups which included:

Indians 56%       Pakistanis 19%    and West Indians 15%

4.26    This area is covered by 5 field teams, based at Walsall (two teams) West Bromwich, Wednesbury and Aldridge. Although the Probation sub-area does not correspond exactly to the Walsall Borough and comparisons are therefore inadvisable, this sub-area must include the Asian population identified in the Census.

### (a) Walsall:

4.27    Officers comment that despite the sizeable Asian population, the number of Asian clients is always low. The question was posed whether this was a true reflection of the numbers appearing before the courts and whether the incidence of crime within this ethnic group is very low. There were only 6 Asians on caseload at this office, all young people and all subject to custodial sentences (5 Detention Centre and 1 Borstal).

4.28    Although the West Indian community is significantly smaller than the Asian community there were 16 West Indian clients, 11 subject to supervision orders. (7 on Probation Orders and 4 under C. & Y.P. Supervision).

4.29    There is therefore a marked difference in the nature of contact between these two ethnic groups. Further exploration, possibly a court survey, is being considered.

### (b) West Bromwich:

4.30    All officers share in the supervision of 34 black clients. Officers who have worked in this area for a long time and have built up considerable cultural knowledge related to the area comment that this is an area with a changing profile. A few years ago it was the scene of activity amongst young West Indians. There has been a distinct decline in the number of young black people coming before the courts and it is thought that West Indian parents have integrated with the white community and many of the young black people who have left home have moved to other areas. There are some Rastafarians mostly concentrated in two roads who link with the Handsworth Rastafarian groups.

4.31    The Asians in this area do not have independent communities and are fragmented having ties with either Smethwick or Handsworth.

### (c) Wednesbury:

4.32    This is the neighbouring office to West Bromwich yet with only 6 black clients. The complexities of the few cases which arise were pointed out and

the need expressed for changes in methods of supervision and the wider use of community resources.

### (d) Aldridge:

4.33 There are very few black residents in this area and none under supervision at the present time, but there are officers here with cultural experience and interest.

### Birmingham North (Probation Sub Area D)

| Category of Supervision | Total on area caseload | No. & % of ethnic minorities on caseload | |
|---|---|---|---|
| Probation | 280 | 52 | (18.6%) |
| C. & Y.P. Supervision | 240 | 72 | (30.0%) |
| Suspended Sentence Supn. | 22 | 1 | (4.5%) |
| Money Payment Supn. | 5 | 3 | (60.0%) |
| Detention Centre Licence | 52 | 17 | (32.7%) |
| Borstal Licence | 54 | 30 | (55.5%) |
| Prison Licence | 34 | 15 | (44.0%) |
| Parole | 41 | 13 | (13.7%) |
| Voluntary After-Care | 95 | 35 | (36.8%) |
| Pre-release | 299 | 53 | (17.7%) |
| Matrimonial & Wardship | 282 | 86 | (30.5%) |
| Kindred Social Work | 67 | 13 | (19.4%) |
| **TOTAL** | **1471** | **390** | **(26.5%)** |

4.34 There is particular concern in Birmingham North for the situation of the young black people referred to in other sections of this report. The social problems, noticeably lack of employment and accommodation, have been heightened by the movement of Afro/Caribbeans to this area during recent years (eg, as confirmed by West Bromwich officers) who have linked to the Rastafarian and other black groups in the area, indeed Handsworth may be considered 'one of the capitals of ethnic minority communities'.

4.35 Birmingham CRC have identified between 300 and 400 Rastafarians in the area, a picture which is being repeated in other parts of the country but not in any other area of West Midlands County.

4.36 The area is covered by 7 field teams. Newton Street (in the City Centre – two teams), Perry Barr (four teams) and Sutton Coldfield a single team. Officers from both Newton Street and Perry Barr offices point to the considerable difficulties faced in working from large office blocks which are not situated within the local communities which they serve. This is of particular importance to the black communities who develop strong local networks and the Probation Offices cannot be readily seen to be part of them. The statistics point to the very low proportion of black clients on suspended sentence supervision in marked contrast to the much higher proportion of black clients on Borstal, Detention Centre and Prison Licence, and on Voluntary After-Care.

4.37    **Perry Barr** is the office engaged in working with the largest number of black clients in the County (302) of which 231 are West Indians and 41 Asians. **Newton Street** officers have also been engaged in working with black clients over a long period as this office covers some of the oldest areas of settlement (eg, Winson Green and Ladywood). Officers share the supervision of 52 West Indians and 7 Asians.

4.38    **Sutton Coldfield** is a single team office on the county boundary and currently supervises only 4 West Indian clients but officers comment that there is movement of black families out of Handsworth into Kingstanding and therefore a likelihood that work with black clients may increase gradually if redistribution continues.

4.39    There are long serving officers, many with considerable experience of multi-racial social work throughout this area. It is particularly noticeable that new officers have to develop their skills and knowledge in this field of work rapidly and considerable interest is shown in it. All officers assigned to this area can expect to be working with black clients.

4.40    Resources have been strained and action taken by Police, Social Services, Probation and other agencies have been preventative measures and initiatives to alleviate the situation. Some are aimed specifically at black people, (ie, Handsworth Alternatives Scheme outlined in detail in 'Linked Projects'), yet in all areas of work in which officers are engaged black people will play a significant part.

4.41    Illustrations of initiatives in Birmingham North include:

(i)    The North West Parents' Association, a Group, meeting monthly for talks and discussions on such topics as 'Your Child and: the Law; Employment; School; etc', is open to all parents of clients but the composition of the Group is mainly West Indian.

(ii)    One team has undertaken a project to create a much needed resource. By linking with Adulum Homes, a property has been acquired to be used by the young single homeless, maximum stay 12 months, with the Probation Officers taking responsibility for their own clients and working towards obtaining long term accommodation.

(iii) The large groups of Voluntary Associates include approximately 32 black volunteers who are mainly West Indians, active in a variety of ventures.

(iv) A NACRO sponsored Youth Opportunities Programme has been operating in Handsworth since September 1978, offering work experience to young offenders (aged 17-19) and has made a considerable contribution towards placing young black people in permanent work.

(v) Harambee Hostel, which is essentially for the young black single homeless person, is a valuable resource accepting referrals from agencies in any area and the Probation Service is linked by a liaison Probation Officer and a Senior Probaton Officer on the House Committee.

(vi) A senior officer is currently studying for an M.Phil. at Bradford University on 'Race and Sentencing'.

(vii) Other officers are engaged in a variety of projects and undertakings, ie. Secretary of Handsworth Law Centre, Involvement with Lozells Police Project and Holyhead School and Community Centre.

4.42    The Area has produced two training days on West Indian Culture and officers and volunteers contribute towards a variety of Training Courses.

## Birmingham West (Probation Sub Area E)

| Category of Supervision | Total on area caseload | No. & % of ethnic minorities on caseload | |
|---|---|---|---|
| Probation | 260 | 15 | (5.8%) |
| C. & Y.P. Supervision | 74 | 13 | (17.8%) |
| Suspended Sentence Supn. | 19 | — | — |
| Money Payment Supn. | 2 | — | — |
| Detention Centre Licence | 26 | 6 | (23.1%) |
| Borstal Licence | 32 | 5 | (15.6%) |
| Prison Licence | 31 | 6 | (19.4%) |
| Parole | 26 | 3 | (11.5%) |
| Voluntary After-Care | 117 | 5 | (4.3%) |
| Pre-release | 424 | 20 | (4.7%) |
| Matrimonial & Wardship | 181 | 19 | (10.5%) |
| Kindred Social Work | 49 | — | — |
| **TOTAL** | **1241** | **92** | **(7.4%)** |

4.43    This sub-area has no readily identifiable black communities but the number of individual black families (mainly West Indian) within the area appears to be increasing gradually. The area is covered by 5 field teams based at Kent Street (City Centre – two teams), Selly Oak (two teams), Harborne (single team) who collectively supervise 92 black clients.

### (a) Kent Street:

4.44    Kent Street houses the After-Care Unit which deals primarily with people of no fixed abode. Those in contact will already have personal and economic problems and there is a high incidence of mental disorder amongst people assisted by this office. Most of these clients could be said to be 'hard to place' in both accommodation and employment and the additional cultural factors to be taken into account often adds to the problems.

4.45    The Asian community in general provides the structure and contacts for the support of its members which West Indian culture lacks. It is therefore the West Indian homeless ex-offender who needs the greatest support from the Service (26 West Indian – 1 Asian clients). Accommodation and employment are high priorities. Officers stress the need for assistance and resources to meet the needs of this black group.

### (b) Selly Oak:

4.46    Officers at Selly oak had not fully realised the number of black people under supervision and had thought the number to be much less (22 West Indians – 8 Asians). In this office the widest range of attitudes towards work with black people was encountered and there is a diversity of views regarding the necessity for training or special attention to be given to this dimension of work.

### (c) Harborne:

4.47    Officers here were interested in exploring the process of integration which is taking place and the difficulties which had been experienced in the introduction of young black clients (10 West Indians) into predominantly white groups such as an Intermediate Treatment group. Resources were sought for an activity centre for young people which it was thought would attract both black and white young people.

### Birmingham East (Probation Sub Area F)

4.48    This area is covered by 5 field teams based at Saltley (four teams) and Newton Street (City Centre – single team). Black groups under supervision at Saltley include 98 West Indians, 28 Pakistanis and 7 Indians and at

34

Newton Street 12 West Indians, 5 Indians and 2 Pakistanis.

| Category of Supervision | Total on area caseload | No. & % of ethnic minorities on caseload | |
|---|---|---|---|
| Probation | 183 | 15 | (8.2%) |
| C. & Y.P. Supervision | 189 | 37 | (19.6%) |
| Suspended Sentence Supn. | 29 | 2 | (6.9%) |
| Money Payment Supn. | — | — | — |
| Detention Centre Licence | 60 | 12 | (20.0%) |
| Borstal Licence | 67 | 14 | (20.9%) |
| Prison Licence | 38 | 2 | (5.3%) |
| Parole | 31 | 9 | (29.0%) |
| Voluntary After-Care | 75 | 30 | (40.0%) |
| Pre-release | 298 | 26 | (8.7%) |
| Matrimonial & Wardship | 213 | 34 | (15.9%) |
| Kindred Social Work | 58 | 4 | (6.9%) |
| **TOTAL** | **1241** | **185** | **(14.9%)** |

4.49 The black communities stretch across the border between Birmingham East and Birmingham South and the composition of the population is similar. The number of black people under supervision is almost identical in these two areas yet Birmingham East is one quarter the size of Birmingham South. The teams engaged in covering the Inner City areas supervise most of the black clients in this concentrated area. There is a large Pakistani community in Saltley and West Indians mainly reside in the Newtown area which borders on Lozells and Handsworth.

4.50 In 1973, a Birmingham Inner Area Study focused on Small Heath aimed at defining the Inner Areas problems, investigating methods of improving the environment, looking at the advanges of greater co-ordination of local services and making recommendations for changes in methods of approaching Inner City problems. This area was found to have poor recreational facilities, and was in need of a means of providing comprehensive advice to the community. The clearance and redevelopment programme was urged to take into account the needs of the residents. Possibly as a result of this study certain community schemes developed in this area.

4.51 The Small Heath School & Community Centre has offered a massive contribution to the community and is used by all community groups. Probation Officers have taken advantage of a weekly evening course in Asian Studies.

4.52   Some officers comment that they feel there is potential for greater contact with the black communities through the Community Centre and that it is for officers to take initiatives in this direction.

4.53   In Saltley a number of officers are actively engaged in supporting Community ventures such as at St Saviour's Youth and Community Association (where Community Service workers are assisting in the renovations of the church hall), Hutton Hall and Norton Hall. All these ventures are multi-racial and the policy of Birmingham East Probation Service has been to support community initiatives.

4.54   A Home Office sponsored Action Centre serves the black communities in this area and officers comment that it is not the policy of the centre to overidentify with statutory agencies.

4.55   Each team has a group of voluntary associates attached to it which includes 5/6 black volunteers in total. Their particular knowledge is highly valued.

## Birmingham South (Probation Sub Area G)

| Category of Supervision | Total on area caseload | No. & % of ethnic minorities on caseload | |
|---|---|---|---|
| Probation | 307 | 41 | (13.4%) |
| C. & Y.P. Supervision | 195 | 28 | (14.4%) |
| Suspended Sentence Supn. | 29 | 3 | (10.3%) |
| Money Payment Supn. | 2 | — | — |
| Detention Centre Licence | 75 | 19 | (25.4%) |
| Borstal Licence | 38 | 24 | (63.2%) |
| Prison Licence | 35 | 12 | (34.3%) |
| Parole | 21 | 11 | (52.4%) |
| Voluntary After-Care | 86 | 20 | (23.3%) |
| Pre-release | 435 | 36 | (8.3%) |
| Matrimonial & Wardship | 296 | 38 | (12.8%) |
| Kindred Social Work | 53 | 2 | (3.8%) |
| **TOTAL** | **1572** | **234** | **(14.9%)** |

4.56   This area is covered by 7 field teams based at Stratford Road (four teams) Kings Heath, Solihull and Chelmsley Wood (single teams).

### (a) Stratford Road:
4.57   There are 93 West Indians, 30 Pakistanis, and 9 Indians under supervision in this office. This area has the highest number of clients of mixed racial

origins in the county (ie, 33). Parentage was detailed mainly as:

Irish/Pakistani, English/Pakistani, English/West Indian and Pakistani/ Greek

4.58 The main problem identified by officers is communication with Urdu speaking Muslims (Pakistanis). One team covering the section of the area with the highest Pakistani population has approached this difficulty by engaging in a Regional Staff Development Project of their own design which includes tuition in Urdu for 1 hour per week, use of a consultant from Birmingham CRC and two team training days. They do not foresee themselves reaching the point where they will be able to interview in Urdu but taken as a whole, the project is focused on building communication bridges and developing cultural understanding. Members say it is proving effective and is giving increased confidence in contact with Urdu speaking people. Representatives of other office teams have joined this team for this project but it was not possible to accommodate all who wanted to take part. This team would like to pursue an advanced workshop at a later date in order to apply the knowledge gained to the cultural implications of their work. One member of the team is visiting India at her own initiative and sees this as another dimension which can be added for the benefit of the team. Another development from this project also of interest to other teams, is making closer contact with the local communities and religious centres and increasing the use of black volunteers, already a valuable resource.

4.59 West Indians are scattered throughout this area and are evenly distributed on caseloads. There has been concern expressed at the groups of West Indian youths who gather on the street corners due to unemployment, who appear to have no constructive activity. There is also comment that it appears to be housing policy to accommodate West Indian unsupported mothers in high rise blocks which it is suggested is hard-to-let property.

4.60 There are no moves towards officers taking any collective action. One comment which brought general agreement was: 'West Indians keep a very low profile. They cause me no problems, the question is, "Am I a problem for them?"'.

4.61 Working with clients of mixed racial origins was mentioned in most groups and the complexity of cases in which the culture 'clash' involves three cultures was expressed. This was particularly evident in domestic cases involving custody and access issues, and amongst teenagers seeking their own cultural identity.

### (b) Kings Heath:

4.62 All officers are conscious of working in a 'fringe' area where the composition of residents might change at any time, particularly dependent upon housing policies. The Wives' Group has proved interesting, giving cultural learning experiences both to its members and officers as it includes West Indian mothers and their children. The group has been on holiday together and officers spoke of the opportunity to learn of the different patterns of child care which allowed for them to see the positive side of other cultural practices. Some racial prejudices were aired but the residential situation allowed for this to be dealt with and cross cultural relationships developed.

### (c) Chelmsley Wood:

4.63 This team has the disadvantage of being geographically isolated in a large, relatively new housing development which is still in the process of forming its own identity. There are very few Asian residents but a number of West Indians who in the main are families with children of school age. The West Indian youths form into cultural sub-groups in their leisure time. This is an area where social/economic factors will have significance for the young generation, and officers are aware that the content and nature of their work could well change considerably during the coming years.

### (d) Solihull:

4.64 The few residents from black groups appear to be in the professional classes, and may have entered into a 'mixed' marriage. Officers have identified involvement in some domestic cases in this category. Officers here have already had cultural experience in other areas or living abroad and there is a high interest in cultural aspects of work as they say they wish to 'keep abreast of thinking and developments'.

4.65 Birmingham South have organised 2 Area Training Days during 1979, one on Asian culture and one on West Indian culture, the aim being to introduce *all* officers to the cultural aspects of work and enable them to examine their own attitudes towards different cultures. 32 officers attended out of a possible 45. Those who did not attend were thought to be officers who were not engaged in working with black people at that time.

### Coventry (Probaton Sub Area H)

4.66 The population of Coventry is approximately 320,000 out of which approximately 25,000 residents are black. The Asian communities are centred in the Foleshill District. Coventry City Council in 1977 produced the Foleshill District Plan which pays particular attention to the needs of the Asian communities:

| Category of Supervision | Total on area caseload | No. & % of ethnic minorities on caseload | |
|---|---|---|---|
| Probation | 280 | 16 | (5.7%) |
| C. & Y.P. Supervision | 58 | 3 | (5.2%) |
| Suspended Sentence Supn. | 12 | — | — |
| Money Payment Supn. | 13 | — | — |
| Detention Centre Licence | 57 | 9 | (15.8%) |
| Borstal Licence | 49 | 5 | (10.2%) |
| Prison Licence | 23 | 8 | (34.8%) |
| Parole | 23 | — | — |
| Voluntary After-Care | 52 | 9 | (17.3%) |
| Pre-release | 311 | 13 | (4.2%) |
| Matrimonial & Wardship | 63 | 10 | (15.9%) |
| Kindred Social Work | 12 | 1 | (8.3%) |
| **TOTAL** | **953** | **74** | **(7.8%)** |

'Most British people would not expect newcomers to change their religion, what they eat or how they dress, but everyone should have the chance to get a job and a house. This does not happen and there are certain groups of people, and particularly coloured people, who still have greater difficulties in getting jobs. A third of those who were unemployed in Foleshill in 1976 were coloured and a study of school leavers in 1976 showed that they were twice as likely as others to be unemployed. Employed coloured people are often in low-paid positions because they are unskilled or their qualifications are not recognised in Britain and as a result they can only afford cheaper housing in the sort of areas which often do not have many other facilities. However, most of the problems of the coloured people in an area like Foleshill are the same as the other people living there: employment, housing and money. All the issues raised in Foleshill are community relations issues and ways of reducing these problems will help everyone in Foleshill. A social survey showed that 12% of households had at least one person who spoke little or no English and many of these are women.'

4.67   Problems, therefore, have been identified as social and economic and that of communication. The employment situation appears to be particularly serious for West Indian youth, many of whom would be British born. Officers speak of 'disaffected West Indian youth' and of the collective approach made by Coventry City Council but there is still cause for serious concern at the lack of opportunities for this group.

4.68    The area is served by four district teams and a community service unit all operating from the centre of the city. Some teams cover patches with a higher concentration of black residents than others. 21 officers share the supervision of 73 black clients. An Asian officer supervises 17 Indian clients out of a total of 23. This has been deliberate policy to the extent that he speaks a number of Asian languages and is familiar with the cultural considerations involved but it is not anticipated that he will continue to take responsibility for such a proportion of Asian clients.

4.69    A Senior Probation Officer and 3 Probation Officers form a small interest group who have initiated a Training Day with the assistance of Coventry CRC attended by the majority of officers. This group hopes to stimulate interest and racial awareness amongst colleagues and to act as an officer resource.

4.70    The Probation Service is represented on Coventry CRC and its Social Services Panel. In October 1979 the CRC were debating the numbers and positions of juveniles appearing before the courts and the Service was asked whether we were able to quantify the percentage of work with members of ethnic minority groups in relation to the numbers appearing before the Courts. We were not able to provide this information in response to a question which has also been asked in other areas and it may be an important one to explore.

4.71    Coventry has a few black volunteers amongst its large group of voluntary associates and a gentleman with special knowledge of cultural and linguistic skills who is of invaluable assistance. Further recruitment of black volunteers, their use and training needs is under consideration.

4.72    The Community Service Unit is also reviewing the use of Community Service Orders for black offenders.

**Ethnic Minorities Liaison and Advisory Group**

4.73    In December, 1978, a working party was convened at the request of County Management, to consider and advise management about the proposed post of Adviser on Ethnic Minorities and to prepare a job description.

4.74    Each Assistant Chief Probation Officer's area had been asked to nominate a member who was interested in ethnic minority matters. The group completed its task after three meetings. It was recommended that the group continue to meet and was re-convened by Assistant Chief Probation

Officer (Training), who had also been designated to take responsibility at management level for the work of the Ethnic Minorities Adviser.

4.75 The group therefore consists of ten members (eight area representatives, ACPO (Training) and Adviser) and meets on average once every 6 weeks. Initially it was unclear how this group would develop and on 23rd November, 1979, EMLAG clarified its own perception of its purpose which was circulated in the minutes of the meeting as follows:

> '*The existence of the group demonstrated the importance attached by WMCPACS to this sphere of work; clearly this in itself was not enough. Nor should it exist only to be a channel for information and a support to the Adviser, though both these aspects had some importance. It was proposed the purpose of the group should be to advise management on the subject of ethnic minorities, to initiate for change when necessary at management and main grade level, and to support others who are taking initiatives as appropriate (eg, Handsworth Alternatives Scheme).*
> '*Concern was expressed lest the EMLAG simply become part of bureaucratic machinery in a rather sterile way. EMLAG members should themselves develop their awareness and knowledge of the important issues. The group should be concerned with matters not only within WMCPACS but beyond on which the Service might or should be prepared to express a view. Such matters might include housing, sentencing of black offenders, "treatment" packages, immigration policies.*
> '*It was suggested that concern re: obtaining information may become over-great but it was agreed that EMLAG (and WMCPACS as a whole) would only be able to speak with authority if views were supported by evidence. It was proposed that EMLAG should identify the important issues facing the Service in its involvement with ethnic minorities and inform itself appropriately in order to speak to the issues.*'

4.76 The primary focus of the work of the Adviser and of this group was confirmed as being with black people, whom it was recognised were in a vulnerable position with the community and whose contact with the legal and penal system had given rise to a number of serious concerns.

# 5. Specialised Services

### Community Service Units

5.1   Community Service as an alternative to a custodial sentence is available throughout the West Midlands County. An offender is sentenced to a specific number of hours service ranging from a minimum of 40 hours to a maximum of 240 hours.

5.2   Selection processes vary from one area to another. However, there are certain categories of offenders which are often regarded as unsuitable for Community Service, such as sex offenders, violent offenders, people who are of no fixed abode, drug addicts, alcoholics. There are no specific instructions against such recommendations but general queries would be raised about their suitablity. It may be that if any particular ethnic group is highly represented in any such category chances of Community Service would be lowered. (Indirect racial discrimination).

5.3   At the 30th November, 1979, 554 orders were operational of which 69 were members of ethnic minority groups. Community Service officers have been discussing a range of factors relating to Community Service in relation to black people. There has now been an opportunity to experience and assess any practical difficulties encountered during the operation of the sentence. From these discussions two main queries arise:

(1) Are there factors militating against selection of black offenders *at any point in the system?*
(2) Are there any cultural factors which occasion difficulty for either the Community Service worker or the Supervisor in the operation of that sentence?

5.4   A Senior Lecturer in Community and Youth work from Westhill College, Selly Oak, is undertaking a Research Project on behalf of Birmingham CSO Team.[1]

---

[1]Paper outlining research proposals – Liz Hoggarth

5.5 Within this comprehensive study certain groups will be selected for detailed examination. This would involve a much closer look at the reasons for discrimination against a particular group; and the conditions that contribute to whether or not they are offered a community service order; and the conditions under which such an order could be viable. Ethnic minority groups will be included in this section. Examples of relevant factors for investigation are given in relation to Asians. 'It seems likely that a low proportion of Asians arrive on Community Service orders. If this is in fact the case, it is possible that there is a general process of racial discrimination operating; but answers to some more precise questions would add to our knowledge of the problem:

> What offences do they commit?
> Do they opt for a Crown Court trial?
> Do they plead quilty or not guilty?
> How do they present themselves when interviewed by a Probation Officer?
> Do religious and cultural factors mean that certain agencies or certain tasks would be unacceptable to them?
> Are there communication/language difficulties?
> Do they experience prejudice from those they meet while doing Community Service? Would that contribute to a low rate of success?
> Or are Asian offenders in fact highly 'successful' on community service?

5.6 These are some of the questions which Probation Officers have been posing and to which this initiative should begin to supply some answers. Officers in the field suggest that it is possible that certain cultural stereotypes are being applied inappropriately.

5.7 For example, in assessing for reliability the assumption may be made that West Indians are less likely to be good time-keepers and therefore may be thought unsuitable for Community Service. This is an extremely important area for investigation as Community Service provides a real alternative to custodial sentences which is readily available. Is it being fully utilised in respect of the black offender?

**Birmingham Community Service Project**

5.8 A Community Service Scheme was started in Birmingham North in May 1978. Community Service workers, with Orders ranging from 40-240 hours, were expected to work two sessions weekly; on Thursday evenings and on Saturday mornings.

5.9 It soon became obvious that most black workers, especially Rastafarians, were failing to keep their second work appointment. We found this was due chiefly to staying up late on Friday night at parties. When they did report, they were often irritable and unco-operative. Most of the Rastafarian clients are unemployed and many request work on weekdays, rather than on Saturday mornings. At the same time, numerous requests were being received from social workers, probation officers, and other community agencies for help with various difficulties caused by lack of transport. It was decided, therefore, to set up a transport group using the old 'Queensway Trust' van to provide a work activity for the unemployed workers. This group became known as the Mobile Task Force (initials M.T.F.). To date, 50 workers (70% of whom were black) with a collective total of 8,000 hours to work, have completed approximately 3,000 hours exclusively on the Mobile Task Force.

5.10 Initially, the M.T.F. consisted of between 2-5 Community Service workers, with the driver as their supervisor, working all day on Thursday. The majority of these offenders were sentenced for motoring offences and minor burglary, although females were nearly all sentenced for shoplifting offences. Their ages range betwen 19 years to 35 years.

5.11 The Thursday session was to start at 10am from the Community Service Office This was not successful, as workers were reporting at irregular times. Due to the irregular start, it was agreed to call for clients at their homes. This, on occasions, meant knocking on doors for five to ten minutes to get a reply and waiting another twenty minutes in the van. This situation improved as the group developed and now it seldom occurs.

5.12 Work sessions were extremely successful. The workers were co-operative, reliable and very hard working once they decided to apply themselves to a given task. They were accepting a firm discipline, especially when visiting other peoples homes. The range of tasks varied from furniture removal for social workers clients, especially those facing eviction, to gardening for the elderly, handicapped, and also minor painting and decorating.

5.13 Some difficulties were anticipated with regard to attitude and commitment of the Rastafarian workers. They are very conscious of the kind of work they are prepared to do, and for whom they are working. With a few exceptions, they have proved to be good workers, efficient and quite resourceful.

5.14 The failure rate with regard to attendance was quite low. This could be attributed to the informal atmosphere facilitated by the mobile scheme, which allowed for sharing and discussion of each others joy and problems. Advice and opinions were given frankly and were normally treated with respect leading to the development of comradeship and companionship. Topics of conversation, and sometimes heated arguments covered such things as motor cars, politics, reggae music ('dread' music), African history and geography, relationships with Police, life in Remand Institutions, and once even cannibalism. The depths of thought shown in these discussions suggested abilities well beyond those that the clients are often thought to possess.

5.15    A common theme throughout the past two years of the M.T.F. is the feeling held that they were taken to Court too early in their youth for what some considered to be minor misdemeanour or for first time offences. Whilst there might be argument about innocence regarding certain charges, most workers readily accepted their treatment by the police as the main cause of grievance rather than the fact that they had been arrested and charged. There is a high degree of familiarity with the court process. Names of magistrates and judges who they consider to be fair and those they consider to be prejudiced were well known.

5.16    The black workers in particular, enjoyed travelling to various districts within the Birmingham area, particularly visiting the exclusive parts of Sutton Coldfield. Some were quite amazed by the affluence of homes visited in contrast to the squalor of those visited in inner-city areas. There has been no visible sign of resentment of this affluence, on the contrary many were surprised by the cordiality of most people in such areas, having expected hostility. To date, no major adverse incident has occurred, neither have there been complaints of poor behaviour or quality of work; indeed a number of letters have been received commending the groups efforts.

5.17    One interesting project concerned a sick, elderly gentleman in Erdington. He had to be moved from his bedroom upstairs to the downstairs living room, because of the difficulties his arthritic wife had in caring for him. He was totally bedridden and was unable to sit upright. The operation meant them lifting and holding him in a flat position and carrying him downstairs; and some dismantling and reconstruction of furniture. It was a marvellous success, requiring sensitivity and humility from the workers. They were praised by the social worker who was present who was most impressed by the attitude of the Rastafarians.

5.18 Black workers generally assumed that whites from Kingstanding and Erdington are National Front Skinheads; and white clients felt blacks from Handsworth always carried knives. At the beginning of the day's operations, black workers would refuse to talk with any new white worker and some white workers were equally reluctant to communicate. It is now common practice, therefore, for each new worker to be introduced to each member of the group, this helps to break the ice. The days invariably end with everyone being mates, and with a feeling of having been part of a team.

5.19 As a result of these experiences we believe the Mobile Task Force does help to create racial understanding which, in itself, is a valuable service to the community[1].

### Hostels
5.20 West Midlands County Probation and After-care Service is closely associated with five Approved Probation Hostels, four of which are managed by our own Committee and one is under independent management. There is one Bail Hostel although the Probation Hostels also provide places for those on remand. Offenders reside at a Probation Hostel as a condition of the Probation Order.

### (a) Probation Hostels – adult males
5.21 Registers of residents are not marked with ethnic groupings and therefore most information was given by memory. Resident from ethnic minorities were so few in number that this was not difficult.

Of the four hostels accommodating males:–

Hostel A   Has had no Asian resident at all.
Has had one West Indian resident and two taking bail places.

Hostel B   Has one current resident of mixed racial origin who is regarded as Asian by other residents because of his name.
Has had no West Indian residents during the one year it has been open.

Hostel C   Has had one Asian resident who had previously been in care and fostered to a 'white' family.
Has had four West Indian residents during the last year and would expect to have one or two in residence at any one time. During the last four years the hostel has accommodated approximately fifteen West Indians.

[1]Report by E. Hacker, C.S. Assistant

Hostel D   Was unable to quantify different cultures but during the past two years has accommodated approximately ten residents of various ethnic origins.

### (b) Probation Hostel – females (with Children)
5.22   There have been no Asian residents and no referrals for Asian females.

There are usually one or two West Indians at any one time out of seventeen residents.

### (c) Bail Hostel
5.23   During 1979 there were seven residents from ethnic minority groups, mainly West Indians.

### (d) Referrals and Assessment for Probation Hostels
5.24   Hostel staff commented that referrals for Asians were negligible and that they had no control over the numbers of referrals in any category; therefore if numbers of referrals in relation to ethnic minority groups were thought to be low, this matter should be taken up with officers and the courts.

5.25   Cultural factors which might have a bearing on selection at assessment stages were seen as:

(1) The inability or refusal to communicate.
(2) The composition of the residents of the hostel at that time. There was a feeling that large ethnic minority groups might cause conflict when forming into cultural sub-groups.
(3) Two hostels pointed out that they were aware that their residents held strong racist attitudes and felt it was fair to discuss this when interviewing an applicant from an ethnic minority group. Two other hostels felt this should not be discussed at assessment stage but should be dealt with if it arises.

5.26   Illustrations were given of a few applications in respect of black applicants which had been refused, it was thought for reasons other than cultural factors. One probation officer had challenged a refusal on 'racial grounds'.

### (e) Bail Hostel referrals
5.27   There is no assessment process for the bail hostel and referrals are usually made by telephone – often direct from the court duty officer. No information is requested in respect of ethnic origins. The hostel staff feel this is a perfectly satisfactory procedure.

### (f) Ethnic minorities as residents in hostels

5.28 The Bail Hostel and Hostel C. (the hostel regularly taking West Indians), are both in multi-racial areas. Both commented favourably on West Indians as residents. There had been only one West Indian absconsion from the Bail Hostel. The main problem was seen as the 'cultural shock'[1] and the difficulties this presented in coping with the demands of western society. The Warden of Hostel C commented that he found in the main that West Indians were less psychologically disturbed than many of the 'white' residents, that they had offended in their late teens and did not have a history of offences as juveniles. He felt that there had been significant successes amongst the West Indian residents.

5.29 Probation Hostel staff in general identified some conflict of views amongst residents. Some residents make racist speeches and gestures but often they are without substance as cross-cultural relationships develop. Staff take the approach of discussion and self-searching when racist attitudes become evident.

### (g) Probation Hostel – females with children

5.30 It was not felt that there were the same cultural conflicts amongst the females and comment was added that the West Indian residents are very westernised.

### (h) Voluntary Hostels

5.31 The Probation Service also has contact with a variety of voluntary hostels. The representation of black clients in voluntary hostels seems to be considerably higher but this needs further exploration before any conclusions could be drawn.

### Prison Secondment

5.32 There is only one prison situated in the West Midland County – HM Prison, Winson Green, Birmingham.

5.33 The Senior Probation Officers and eight Probation Officers are seconded to the Prison Service to work in the Welfare Department within the Prison, and link into the service structure as part of the Birmingham West Sub-area. All officers working within the Prison are experienced field-work officers.

5.34 There are over 1,000 prisoners concentrated within a small physical area and living and working conditions are extremely difficult due to lack of space and amenities. Tension, stresses and frustrations of prison life are heightened even further by the difficult environmental conditions, contributing to an atmosphere in which prejudices are likely to be expressed both verbally and physically. It is extremely difficult to assess whether race and colour are the root cause of conflicts or whether on occasion they are used as an outlet for frustrations due to other causes. Within the complex network of relationships between prisoners, prison officers and plain clothes staff which includes Welfare Officers, there are a range of attitudes and prejudices as in any section of society, but the effect of such prejudices is probably far more damaging to all concerned. If black prisoners allege racial harrassment Prison Welfare Officers will need considerable support in their dealing with the Prison Service. Unfortunately racism is always possible when someone has the power to inflict their racial prejudices on, and discriminate against, another.

5.35    All officers working within the prison will have a multi-racial caseload and numerous decisions with cultural aspects have to be made daily by prison personnel in which the Probation Officers may well become involved. Basic guidelines are laid down but there is considerable personal discretion and how prison and probation officers use that discretion is of importance, eg. Moslems are required to fast during the period of Ramadan between the hours of sun rise and sun set. They are allowed to do so but decisions have to be taken as to the provision of food and drink during hours when this would normally not be available to prisoners, complaints of discrimination would be possible if all Moslems within the same prison did not receive the same consideration.

5.36    Probation Officers working within H.M.P. Winson Green put cultural training as a high priority for officers based within institutions. Officers who have already taken part in training are finding it of particular benefit, for instance, in interviews with prisoners, understanding must be given to domestic problems which may differ substantially amongst different ethnic groups.

5.37    Prison regulations preclude the Probation Officers working in prisons from bringing in outside interpreters. When interpreters are needed this service is provided by the Education Officer in Winson Green and Two Prison Officers all with a knowledge of Asian languages. There are reservations amongst field work Probation Officers as to whether this is a satisfactory arrangement.

5.38    There is always a group of prisoners awaiting deportation consisting of men from a variety of ethnic groups, mainly the black groups. Due to administrative procedures they are often in custody at the prison for lengthy periods. If they are to be deported following a prison sentence then a Probation Officer will be in contact, otherwise it is likely that they will have no contact with a social agency. Officers are concerned about this group and ask for their situation to be considered and question whether the Probation Service could ensure its services are offered on a voluntary basis.

5.39    Probation Officers within the prison have a minimal contact and have been requested on occasion to deal with matters outstanding regarding property and financial affairs.

5.40    As would be expected, individuals of different cultural groups gravitate towards each other within the prison. Probation officers within the prison have found that they had very different responses when making contact with the Rastafarians. They are aware that the assumption is that Rastafarians will refuse or avoid contact with white people particularly those identified as members of the penal system but many, and one officer says 'most', Rastafarians will communicate in individual situations (and he added, 'often brighten up my day!'). It was suggested that officers need more material regarding background information of the Rastafarian ideology in order to communicate with a greater understanding of their philosophy.

5.41    The prison visitors centre situated opposite the prison is a cosmopolitan meeting place very well used by those waiting to make a prison visit and all take advantage of the facilities offered which includes a play area for children. The prison visitors centre is run by volunteers and a probation officer working in the prison is usually present. There is no racial tension evident here and the only area of concern is the attitude of some of the women visiting Rastafarian prisoners who have made it clear on occasion that they do not want contact with the white organisers and refuse to allow the children to speak to them either. The reason for such attitudes perhaps calls for further exploration.

5.42    Liaison has been established between the Ethnic Adviser and H.M. Prison.

**The Probation Officer in Court**
5.43    Some Areas or Offices run a system whereby a team of officers, or individual officers are permanently on duty in the Courts. This system is operated at Birmingham, Coventry, Wolverhampton, Walsall and Dudley. In the smaller Courts a rota system usually applies so all officers

take their turn at Court duty. Special Court Units cover the Crown Courts and Divorce Courts in Birmingham, Coventry and the West of the County Service. Ancillary workers are also involved in Court work and all officers will attend Court from time to time with clients and to present reports personally.

5.44 The duties of a Court Duty Officer vary within the different kind of complexes and rituals and tradition often determine his approach. Common to all would be the presentation of reports, interviewing and preparing the initial information in respect of reports requested by the Courts, taking results of sentences passed and dealing with a range of queries pertaining to the Court and to the defendant.

5.45 It is comparatively recently that the position and situation of black people appearing before the Courts has come under scrutiny by ourselves as a Service and by other outside bodies. Issues raised in some areas have been controversial and efforts are being made in a variety of ways in order to clarify issues, debate them with Magistracy and Court staff and reach a working understanding of the situation. Such exchanges are particularly important when the Probation Service is involved in assisting in launching new schemes which are likely to affect sentencing patterns (i.e. Handsworth Alternative Scheme) so that they can be used effectively.

5.46 There is a growing acceptance by Probation Officers, Magistrates and Judges that cultural information is relevant and useful in determining sentence.

5.47 Officers already faced with decisions in Social Inquiry Report writing on how much information to present to the Court and how to present it, have the additional cultural factors adding complexity to report writing. Cultural facts alone are not always helpful unless amplified and related to the current situation. For example, it may be insufficient to give the name of a town or village of birth and upbringing when it cannot be known at the time of writing whether the reader will have any conception of the life-style and tradition associated with a particular area of say the West Indies or India, and which could, and often does, affect behaviour when there has been a transition to another culture.

5.48 Whilst it is not acceptable to put forward cultural factors as an excuse for crime, they may provide an understanding of the behaviour which has culminated in an unlawful act. For example, the element of provocation which is taken into consideration in sentencing can often have a cultural perspective. In the Sikh culture a verbal insult to any women in the extended family or even within the wider community group would seldom be left unchallenged and assault or sexual approaches to a woman would be considered extreme provocation and the males may seek to vindicate the family honour by retaliation. Such conflicts can lead to affray or wounding charges involving a number of males from both respective families.

5.49    Officers have drawn attention to prison sentences which may be given to all or several of the males in such cases, leaving households of women and children in an extremely exposed and vulnerable situation which calls for considerable financial, social and community support. In such situations the communication problems are severe.

5.50    Therefore whilst the Courts are in the position where they must uphold the concept that no citizen can be allowed to take the law into his own hands, they also hold the discretion of which factors they take into account when determining sentence. Probation Officers are therefore in a most responsible position in bringing to the Courts notice facts which they believe are relevant and have a bearing on the defendants situation, or emotional condition but particularly in any matters relating to the commission of an offence.

5.51    The black group who have recently attracted the most attention in Court are the Rastafarians. The atmosphere in the Court when Rastafarians appear has sometimes been described as 'tense'. The defendant is often accompanied by a supporting group who may follow the policy of non-acceptance of and non-cooperation with 'white justice' which is pursued in a variety of ways, such as by a refusal to communicate or a show of disrespect for the system by turning their backs to the Bench. This has been particularly noticeable in the Birmingham City Courts, where most of the Rastafarian defendants appear, but similar attitudes have been encountered in the smaller courts. The Court therefore has its difficulties in retaining total impartiality in sentencing in the face of the rejection of the Court system.

5.52    Liz Hogarth writes 'workers who have to deal with these young people are frequently nonplussed at what appears to them as a very bizarre culture and by what they perceive as an aggressive and threatening stance.'[1]

5.53    Probation Officers in Court sometimes encounter difficulties in

---

[1]'The Rastas'. Liz Hogarth. Social Work Today. Vol. Eleven. 27.11.79.

encouraging co-operation in the preparation of Social Inquiry Reports but report that the information required is usually forthcoming.

5.54 Many officers express the view that the behaviour in Court of the young black offender is often misinterpreted by those who do not recognise the different forms of cultural behaviour and responses, particularly reactions to stress and anxiety. (i.e. a West Indian defendent may smile or even laugh under stress which could be interpreted as insolence, a lack of respect of the Court or unconcern about his position). Interpretations of a defendent's behaviour in Court may be reflected in sentencing.

5.55 Racist remarks are heard at all levels within the legal and penal system including Magistracy and the Judiciary, some of which have been challenged by probation officers. Scrupulous attention needs to be paid in this respect as such remarks are a discredit to the system and maybe the forerunner of discriminatory practices.

5.56 In 1978 St. Basil's Centre, a voluntary organisation in Birmingham, employed a detached youth worker to work with black youth with a focus on those who appear before the Birmingham City Courts. The assistance that this youth worker has given to black youths before the Courts and to their families is considerable. He stood bail on over 100 occasions and ensured the attendance of the defendant back in Court and has been referred to as a 'one man bail hostel'. He has been maligned by many, his achievements received scant recognition in some quarters, possibly because of his outspoken approach and adherence to his beliefs and principles. There is clearly a need for such workers within the legal penal system and the Probation Service can only benefit by their continued involvement in this capacity.

# 6. Linked Projects

6.1     This chapter describes four projects serving ethnic minority clients.

### Handsworth Alternatives Scheme

6.2     The Handsworth Alternatives Scheme is operating to provide a service through Probation Officers to the Courts in Birmingham to assist with the treatment of young black offenders in the 17-25 age range, by harnessing community resources and facilities to provide a range of credible and more acceptable support services to young black people.

6.3     The idea for the scheme arose from concern expressed by Probation Officers working in Birmingham North about the quality and effectiveness of the service which they were providing to the young black people in their area. They were questioning the recommendations made in Officers Reports to the Courts and were concerned about overall quality of justice for this particular client group. A survey conducted by a Senior Probation Officer working in Handsworth[1] provided evidence that such concern was justified and the scheme was set in motion by officers who were pressing for positive action.

6.4     The scheme became operational on the 1st April 1979, and has been funded for a three-year period by the aid of a Home Office Grant. The National Association for the Care and Resettlement of offenders (NACRO) carry the responsibility for the proper and legal administration of the grant and for the staff and premises. The day to day supervision of the project is delegated to a local management committee, consisting of representatives from the Probation Service, NACRO, Birmingham Community Relations Council, Judicary and four Universities.

6.5     The HAS Staff Team (all young black workers) consists of a Co-ordinator, two Development Officers and a Clerical Officer. They provide advice and practical help with accommodation, employment, education, recreation, and a high level of social support. HAS hopes eventually to provide support for two hundred people annually.

---

[1]Ethnic Minorities, P. D. Whitehouse, SPO.

6.6 The HAS Staff also have a development function. Many of the support facilities either do not exist or are not readily accessible or acceptable to the group in question. The Team are therefore working to smooth the problems of access to existing facilities and where there are gaps in the provision to work to set up new facilities.

ACCOMMODATION – to provide a range of accommodation facilities for 50 people annually from Local Authority and Housing Association resources.

EMPLOYMENT – to generate work preparation and job opportunities from the Careers Service and Manpower Services Commission resources; improve access in YOP and STEP Schemes.

EDUCATION – to develop a range of educational opportunities in the local authority network, the WEA and other bodies. HAS has appointed a Robert Kennedy fellow to specialise in remedial education.

RECREATION – To develop with other groups a range of sporting, musical and adventure facilities.

SOCIAL SUPPORT – Aiming to involve black people as volunteer associates with the programme.

6.7 The Scheme will be monitored and evaluated and the results will be published by NACRO at the end of the project. The HAS Team work in partnership with Probation Officers and is also available to assist Probation Officers in the preparation of Social Enquiry Reports, particularly when there is a risk of the offender attracting a custodial sentence.

6.8 The Scheme is also concerned to assist with the resettlement of young people returning to the area from penal establishments and young people considered to be at risk. HAS are hoping to win the confidence of the Courts and Magistrates have visited the Scheme and the signs are very hopeful that it is being viewed as an aid to sentencing and that increasing use will be made of it. The Scheme is publicised in a NACRO leaflet 'An Invitation to Refer'.

6.9 The main query about HAS has been, 'Why the focus on Handsworth?'. The answer is simply because:

(a) At this stage the need is great in this area, and
(b) Officers have communicated that need and combined with Management and other bodies to take action.

6.10 That such action is experimental is undeniable and one reservation that many officers have is that, 'grandiose' new schemes will have little better effect than traditional methods. In relation to Handsworth Alternatives Scheme, such comment can neither be proved nor disproved as the action is to stimulate a situation in which more of the young blacks appearing before the Court can reach probation officers who must then, in the current climate in Handsworth, be seen to have more practical and concrete offerings than are available to them in the prevailing social/economic situation and be able to communicate with those who are withdrawing from contact with 'the system' and the 'white community'.

6.11 Probation Officers are unanimous in their agreement that it is increasingly difficult to assist in finding employment and housing, and dealing with the financial problems of the homeless unemployed are complex and time consuming. This imaginative scheme offers a resource to the probation officer in:

(a) Widening his sphere of realistic recommendations, to include supervision, with or without conditions which he may not previously have thought viable.
(b) Offering additional avenues of communication with probationers through Handsworth Alternative Schemes workers.
(c) Enabling joint planning and shared intervention.

6.12 Handsworth Alternatives Scheme does not pull its punches. From the wording of the introductory document objectives are stated forcefully. HAS staff have not waivered from that stance. Some officers feel there has been a deliberate attempt to challenge their credibility in working with black people at all. It has also been suggested that the message of the Service in linking with a project in which black workers are involved is a move towards a separatist policy of matching black worker to black client. This is definitely not the Service's policy in general but the probation officer who works with a black colleague may learn a great deal in regard to approach and methods of communication in exactly the same way as suggested in 'Volunteers', ie, working with an Asian volunteer.

6.13 The argument that positive discrimination for black ultimately discriminates against white has been put forward. Officers are reminded of the Race Relations Act, 1976 which allows special provision to be made to meet certain special needs for particular ethnic groups and permit certain kinds of positive action, which clearly covers the situation in Handsworth at this time. As a Service, society would say that we discriminate in favour of the offender in the provisions we attempt to make for his welfare. It is a small step only to make additional provision for the black offender, or even potential offender.

6.14    Since talking with the Handsworth Alternative Scheme team, the Adviser has consistently backed this project, recommending that officers should test the credibility of the service it offers, by referring any appropriate cases personally, thus being in a position to make their own assessments and enabling them to add criticism, comments and ideas as consumers of the project.

**Handsworth Project**

6.15    In 1977 the Probation Service was giving serious thought to a variety of Projects which could benefit both the Service and the Community and the Handsworth Project and a Day Centre were being considered as possibilities. A working party from within the Service was convened working on the premiss that strategy must be preventative as well as reactive, focusing therefore on Projects which could improve conditions associated with social breakdown and crime.

6.16    The working party report highlighted the work of the Service with culturally and racially alienated groups including the rootless offenders who find refuge in the Inner City Areas. The Service was concerned to reach more closely into the community in the areas where offending behaviour was seen to be most overt.

6.17    Birmingham is one of a limited number of local authorities engaged in an Inner City Partnership Scheme developed to contain and revitalise the Inner City areas which due to a variety of social problems are on the decline. 25% of funding for the schemes is met by Local Authority, 75% by the Home Office

6.18    Technically the Probation Service was not amongst agencies which the Inner City Partnership Funding would assist, but negotiations were successful and funding was agreed for the Handsworth Project and later for a Day Centre.

6.19    It was agreed that a Probation Officer should be 'detached' from the Service to develop the Project and on 1st September 1978, the Project leader was appointed, an Officer already operating in Handsworth thus with ground knowledge of the Area and its residents. The Probation Service is the direct sponsor of the Scheme and is responsible for its management. The Project leader remains accountable to the Service although the term 'detached' Probation Officer implies he is 'attached' elsewhere. It is an intangible concept to be 'detached' from an agency and 'attached' to the community, all the more difficult to establish in this case as for the first twelve months the Project operated from a Probation Office compounding the difficulties in creating an independent identity within the community. The Project now has its own premises.

6.20   Whilst not directly responsible for any form of statutory supervision of offenders the project has provided activities and resources which are available to any members of the local community, including offenders. The emphasis is retained on the prevention of crime by the alleviation of social deprivation and the provision of creative activities.

6.21   The Scheme from September 1978 to December 1979, has included:

(a) **Dance Drama Group**

6.22   The group comprises 16 members aged between 16 and 22 years. It has developed into a serious performing group undertaking at least twenty public engagements during the year including a performance at Hewell Grange Borstal. The aim of the group in addition to public entertainment is to develop confidence, creating new ideas using these skills to assist others from within the community.

6.23   Parents have also been involved in dress-making and other related fields, contact which is encouraged to enable more fruitful understanding between the young and the old to develop.

6.24   Long term plans are for the group to be self-financing and a community project in its own right. Plans include establishing a travel scholarship scheme whereby members of the group will be able to travel and study aspects of Afro-Caribbean art with the expressed wish that they will return to share their knowledge with schools, other young people and the group. Plans are already established for tuition at the Jamaican School of Dance in both dancing and drumming.

(b) **Electronics Group**

6.25   This was designed as a short term course in response to requests from two local schools. It consisted of 4 to 6 members and meetings were held on a weekly basis when topics relating to basic electronics were discussed and simple mathematical problems and work sheets were used. Two members have now begun studying electronics.

### (c) Mother and Babies Group

6.26   Following a street by street survey the Project felt convinced of the desperate need for adequate facilities for the under-fives. Premises were organised at a local school to encourage both parents and schools to see schools as not simply teaching institutions but with a wider role to play in the community. It also offered sixth formers the opportunity to become involved with parents and young children and possibly doing project work. The venue was subsequently changed due to difficulties arising and in February 1979 began operating from Trinity House, Aston. Membership varied between 5-12 mothers with children and the group met twice weekly. Speakers were invited to discuss problems relating to child development and lectures organised by statutory agencies in Handsworth were attended, and day outings organised.

### (d) Training Course

6.27   During April and June 1979, a very successful Training Course was organised and participants came from a diversified background including Social Workers, Magistrates, Probation Officers, Prison Officers, Teachers, Police and members of the community. It offered scope for participants to expand their knowledge, skills and appraise their own attitudes towards their work and every day relationships with individuals from a different cultural background. It is planned that Courses such as this will have a regular slot in the Project Programme.

### (e) Educational Visit to Jamaica

6.28   This visit took place between 6th January and 16th February, 1980. The visiting group comprised 18 members aged between 16 and 22 years. Selection of participants was done through local schools with the assistance of the Educational Department. This encompassed vast sections of the community in fund raising including numerous statutory and voluntary groups and in particular local and national sporting personalities, musicians, artists and poets have lent their support. Contributions were gratefully received from six Trust Funds.

6.29   The visit was organised through the Jamaican High Commission and arrangements were made to visit industry and commerce and participate in school activities, youth clubs and visit the police training department. On return it is planned these experiences will be shared with other groups and schools throughout Birmingham.

6.30   In addition to the actual activities, workers have become involved in a variety of 'one off' situations such as visiting custodial institutions, supporting families through crisis periods, visiting Law Courts with residents, making enquiries and holding meetings with Housing Department, DHSS and Employers.

6.31 Much has been learnt during the Handsworth Project's experimental beginning and future developments can now be based on experience rather than assumption. The acquisition of spacious new premises, including a dance studio and the possibility of an increase of staffing levels opens up wider opportunities. The 'Handsworth Project' is to become known as a 'CULTURAL RESOURCE CENTRE' for the local community which is of particular relevance to young people and which will provide a range of programmes borne out of their interests and aspirations. Both offenders and non-offenders will be welcomed in an effort to reduce the level of crime in Handsworth. The Centre will also be used by the Probation Service and its facilities offered to social workers, teachers and others who are interested in broadening their working methods and becoming involved in some of the activities offered. In this way methods of fieldwork practice which are applicable to multi-racial areas can be explored together with young people and a greater understanding of the locality and its problems should emerge.

6.32 It is planned that at a later date the Handsworth Alternatives Scheme will occupy adjoining premises, thus bring together practical, supportive and creative resources to serve the current needs of the younger members of the community. The aims and objectives of the Centre and the Service are in unison and it is that collective approach which will give this scheme impetus and contribute to its success.

**Activity Centre**
6.33 The establishment of an Activity Centre situated in central Birmingham has been made possible through the Birmingham Inner-City Partnership Scheme, which seeks to achieve, amongst other things, to deal with problems of unemployment and social deprivation amongst sections of the community and to inject new life into deprived areas. Great importance is attached to providing assistance for individuals who suffer from personal and social disadvantages, through the provision of facilities designed to meet those needs and in doing so improve the individual's capacity to function within society and reduce the propensity towards negative, anti-social, and self-defeating behaviour.

6.34 Management of the project is in the hands of the Probation Service, whilst oversight of its overall development falls within the Inner City Partnership programme for Birmingham. The Activity Centre will operate as a multi-purpose sector offering the following facilities:

Work activity, including woodwork, car repair and engineering.
Adult education, including remedial education and social skills training.
Recreational interests.
Community work.
Furniture store.

6.35 The Activity Centre will offer a wide range of activities and interests as a means of enabling individuals to increase their levels of ability and capacity for change. Those affected by long-term unemployment and the inability to avail themselves of employment will be placed in a situation which should allow them to develop new or dormant skills and take an active part in improving their social and personal position in the community. Opportunities for self-improvement through occupational activity and adult education will be offered to the individual in an effort to break patterns of behaviour which might include permanent unemployment, crime or being at odds with oneself and society. Rehabilitation at different levels is, therefore, of importance. Emphasis will be placed on 'learning through doing' to include basic and intermediate tasks that will, progressively, encourage the acquisition of a work habit and the development of social skills.

6.36 The Activity Centre opened on 25 February 1980 to statutory and voluntary social agencies. The catchment area is defined as Birmingham with a special emphasis on the inner city areas. The Centre will be open to both men and women between the ages of 16 and 50 years. Attendance at the Centre will be for a period not exceeding six months, the exact length of stay being determined on an individual basis, subject to such key factors as rate of progress and job availability. Clients attending the Activity Centre will be unemployed and undoubtedly will be in receipt of supplementary benefits. To comply with ruling by the Department of Health & Social Security clients must be considered eligible for employment while in attendance at the Centre. Therefore attendance is based on two days per week so that 20 clients will attend on Monday and Tuesday, whilst a further 20 will attend on Thursday and Friday. Attendance is of a voluntary nature and involves no remuneration to the client.

6.37 In statutory cases the client will attend as a requirement of a probation order though he/she will still be able to take up employment if it becomes available. The requirement within the probation order will read: 'To attend the Activity Centre, Lower Essex St, Birmingham, as directed by the Supervising Officer and whilst attending comply with the instructions given by the Manager of the Activity Centre.'

6.38 The Centre will be staffed by the Manager, Deputy Manager, two Craft Instructors, Receptionist/Typist, professional suprvisors, and volunteers.

6.39 The advent of an Activity Centre in Birmingham offers an opportunity for working in new ways with certain clients; as an experimental project there will be room to extend and modify as necessary. The scope of the project is wide and offers alternative methods of dealing with clients in such a way as to enhance the quality of their lives.

6.40 This new project has been included specifically to show the variety of approaches which are being taken by WMCPACS to alleviate similar social conditions, particularly within the deprived inner city areas.

6.41 In direct contrast to the Handsworth Alternatives Scheme, which is aimed at one disadvantaged group, ie, the young black offender, the Centre offers its facilities and opportunities to the widest possible range of people, which in the centre of Birmingham catchment area will undoubtedly include clients from diverse cultural backgrounds.

6.42 The emphasis is on a positive approach to common problems and the creation of an environment in which individuals can learn new skills together and gain self-confidence.

**Donkey Driving Group**

6.43 In early 1979, a Probation Officer who was at that time liaison officer for Hewell Grange Borstal and who had for some time been involved with donkey driving for the disabled, responded to a request for suggestions for community work projects for the Borstal boys by offering to organise a donkey driving group for the disabled on the estate. The purpose behind the group was that it should be of mutual self-help between the disabled and the lads. The group was set up and became a great success. A waiting list of assistants grew as did the interest of those taking part, and local competitions were entered with this joint venture returning as joint winners from local shows.

6.44 Boys after their release wanted to continue to participate. By this time the Probation Officer had moved to HM Prison, Winson Green and it was in that area that she began to look for facilities for a Birmingham base.

Permission was given to use Hockley Port as a temporary base and the community based group opened in November 1979.

6.45   Hockley is in the centre of a highly multi-racial area and it was therefore a natural development that this group should become a multi-racial group sharing in a new and challenging activity for the area.

6.46   The group is funded by donations from charitable trusts and is hoping to encourage further financial support to enable expansion. Community Service workers are also involved and there are plans for two donkeys to be kept in the Inner City Farm Project.

6.47   This Project has received practical support from the police who have acted as hosts to the Group offering use of the facilities at the Police Riding School and links are being formed with Riding Clubs.

6.48   An Organiser comments 'Donkey Driving must be one of the best possible activities for all ages and types of disabled, including the socially disabled. It is certainly worth seeing how easily those who find difficulty in communicating with people managed to communicate with these amazing animals'.

6.49   This group offers its members rewards and satisfaction in assisting others and presents a different face of authority. Apart from its obvious benefits to a variety of young people it is an exercise in both race and community relations.

7.    **Training and Resources**


**Social Work Training Courses**

7.1    The Central Council for Education and Training in Social Work (CCETSW) draws attention to the importance it attaches to the teaching on CQSW courses in relation to developing a better understanding of people of diverse cultural backgrounds. The Council envisages that teaching will not necessarily be additional but rather that it will be incorporated into existing sequences to include:

(a) Teaching from contributory disciplines.
(b) Teaching about specific characteristics of particular ethnic minorities.
(c) Teaching of social work practice with clients from ethnic minority groups.

7.2    It is the Council's expectation that all three elements will appear in social work training and will be included in curriculum material submitted for recognition and review of CQSW courses. It is recommended that practice placements should include opportunities for direct work with clients drawn from ethnic minority groups whenever possible.


**WMCPACS-Training**

7.3    Training mounted by the West Midlands Probation and After-Care Service to date has been:

(1) Training initiated by sub-areas mainly consisting of staff training days related to specific cultures.
(2) New officers in 1979 received one days introduction to the subject as a part of the first year training programme.
(3) One team is currently engaged in a project of their own design on 'working with Asians' with the assistance of a Consultant from Birmingham Community Relations Council. This also includes tuition in Urdu.
(4) In 1979 the Training Section began developing its own courses and two courses appear in the 1980 programme organised jointly with Birming-

ham Social Services Department for probation officers and social workers.
(a) Working with Asians
(b) Working within the Afro/Caribbean culture.

7.4   Attendance at such courses is not statutory and therefore only officers with a specific interest in this field would be likely to apply.

7.5   A number of Officers have attended Training Courses organised by other bodies. Information from Officers is available so it is possible to gauge the type and level of material which is currently used in training in this field. A considerable amount of information is given, often leaving the recipient to work out the implications for social work practice.

7.6   There is recognition at management level that training is a priority area for development in this area of work but before the Service enters into any expansion in this field, it is vital to determine:

(a) The existing level of cultural knowledge and expertise of Officers.
(b) Attitudes of Officers towards different types of training.
(c) Ways or raising the level of interest in cultural training.
(d) Cultural training needs in relations to local ethnic groups.
(e) The order of priority in relation to other work.

7.7   Attitudes of individual Officers towards training are so variable that formulating Training Programmes presents numerous difficulties. Examples of this are:

(a) Some Officers in multi-racial areas say that they have had to learn by experience, 'by being thrown in at the deep end', and see this as being more valuable than 'sitting behind a desk'. They would advise Officers to learn from their clients and would not take advantage of organised training. They see making errors as an inevitable part of the learning process even if the client is initially disadvantaged by it.
(b) Other Officers believe that all Officers in multi-racial areas should receive comprehensive cultural information on appointment and additional training in race relations and social work with ethnic groups at the earliest opportunity. Comment was made on the burden of responsibility on the experienced officer in passing on a working knowledge to the new officer who has had little previous cultural contact or experience.
(c) Initiatives are being taken by Officers who believe that they must take

personal responsibility for equipping themselves to the best of their ability and may ask for financial support and time allocation to allow them to do so.

7.8    Many Officers in the 'fringe' areas who only occasionally work with black people recognise their lack of cultural knowledge and are unable to reach it through their immediate locality, thus cannot build up a knowledge base through experience and contact with the community.

7.9    Several office teams came to the conclusion that if any member of the team was particularly interested in training to work with ethnic minorities it was a viable proposition providing he would be prepared to share his knowledge with the team. There are a number of Officers in this situation interested in multi-cultural work and comment was frequently made that Officers change their location and therefore need to be prepared for work with all races. Also the composition of ethnic groups in any area is likely to change.

7.10   The way in which information is communicated is considered of paramount importance. Illustration has been given by Officers who have built feelings of resentment against those who they feel, use insensitive training methods. Courses which have taken a workshop approach with participation, allowing for the exploration of attitudes and relationships have the highest success rating from Officers.

**Future Training Plans and ways of developing
a better understanding of cross-cultural social work**
7.11   A range of ideas are being explored from which a comprehensive cultural training programme can be developed.

(a) An introduction to the importance of cultural awareness in social work and basic cultural information through written material.
(b) Developing training courses which will include teaching from contributory disciplines, offering information relating to specific characteristics of particular ethnic groups and relating this to social work practice.
(c) Developing workshops to enable the more experienced Officers to explore methods of working with black people or to focus on detailed aspects of a culture in relation to our work.
(d) Approaching Training Officers and Course Planners to encourage the inclusion of a cultural dimension to a variety of courses.
(e) Development of a Cultural Experience Programme linking with religious centres and black organisations, who are interested in the idea

of providing experience within a cultural setting, allowing for closer communication and cultural learning between groups of people. WMCPACS plans to offer this programme to magistrates, judges, court personnel and students on placement within the service.

(f) Encouragement and support for Area Teams and individuals who are taking initiatives for training in this field.

(g) Combining with other agencies to assist in the development of inter-disciplinary training.

(h) Planning exchange visits between officers in WMCPACS and Probation Services abroad.

7.12    The following are suggestions of the main areas for exploration for Probation Officers engaging in cross-cultural social work:

A. **Background Knowledge**

(a) Historical Information
(b) Geographical Information
(c) Patterns of Migration
(d) Areas of Settlement in UK
(e) General Political Situation
(f) Recognition of Ethnic Minority Groups
(g) Religious Practices
(h) Cultural Figures of Importance – past and present
(i) Introduction to Cultural ('black') Literature
(j) Ceremonies and Rituals

B. **Communication**

(a) Terminology
(b) Different Language Patterns
(c) Non-verbal Communication (body language)
(d) Cultural Communication through the Arts (drama, music, poetry, literature and art)
(e) Cross-cultural Communication – The Different Expectations
(f) Rituals and Greetings
(g) Expression of Emotion (including the use of humour)
(h) The use of Interpreters and how to communicate through a third person

## C. Human Growth and Development

Cultural Patterns in:
(a) Child Rearing Practices
(b) Family Structure – Roles and Dynamics
(c) Social Systems
(d) Cultural Adaptation
(e) Diet
(f) Health and Hygiene
(g) Cultural Stress Patterns
(h) Cultural Aspects of Psychiatric Problems

## D. Racial Advantage/Disadvantage

(a) Stereo-typing/Assumptions/Labelling Process
(b) Prejudice and Discrimination
(c) Race as a Factor in Social Work Practice
(d) The Social and Economic Situation of Ethnic Minority Groups
(e) How it feels to live as a member of a minority group (ie, to be 'black' in a predominantly white society).

## E. Meeting the General Needs of Ethnic Minorities, and Provision for Special Needs in:

(a) Education
(b) Accommodation
(c) Employment
(d) Social Skills
(e) Language Tuition
(f) Recreation and Leisure

## F. The Law Relating to Ethnic Minorities

(a) Race Relations Act 1976 (Including the legal resonsibilities of Social Workers under the terms of the Act).
(b) Immigration Act 1968 (Including issues relating to Immigration, Repatriation, Deportation, Rights of Entry, Rights of Settlement, etc).

## G. Use of Resources

(a) A Knowledge of Central Resources (eg, International Social

Services, Immigrants Advisory Service, Law Centres, etc)

(b) Knowledge of Local Ethnic Minority Communities

(c) Knowledge of Local Resources (Self-help Groups, Resource and Advice Centres for Ethnic Minorities, etc)

(d) Use of Volunteers from Ethnic Minority Groups.

H. **Consideration of Casework and Alternatives to Casework in Relation to Clients from Ethnic Minority Groups**

(a) Consideration of Sentencing Options

(b) One-to-One Supervision

(c) Groupwork

(d) Family Counselling

(e) Projects to Meet Special Needs

(f) Community Work

(g) Community Service

(h) Multi-facility Schemes

(i) Supervision through a Third Person, ie, Volunteer

(j) Hostel Accommodation, eg, Harambee, Hostels for Asian Girls, etc

(k) Special Requirements of Probation Orders.

I. **Custodial Sentences and Through-Care**

(a) Special Difficulties of Ethnic Minorities in Custody

(b) Cultural Aspects of Family Care

J. **Having Regard to all the Foregoing, The Development of Cross-Cultural Social Work Skills in:**

(a) Interviewing

(b) Assessment

(c) Diagnosis

(d) Recommendations – Court Reports

(e) Presentation of Cultural Information in Court Reports.

**Officers with Specialised Knowledge and Experience**

7.13   There are far more Officers within the West Midlands County than have been formally recognised who have considerable knowledge and expertise in this area of work.

7.14   There are Officers who have travelled extensively, have lived or worked abroad, or served in HM Forces abroad. others have identified an interest in cultural aspects of work and have set out to develop it by involvement in the different ethnic communities, enjoying a multi-cultural social life, and taking on further education in culture, languages and race relations.

7.15    Such officers have respresented WMCPACS at Conferences and meetings, have written papers, initiated the setting up of Schemes, Projects, Leisure Activities, Group Work and Research.

7.16    More Officers are now coming forward who are willing to contribute more widely, these officers express the need for:

(1) The interchange of information and ideas across the County and nationally with the opportunity to meet and discuss with others committed to work in this field.
(2) Specialised training workshops to allow exploration of special issues or areas of work at greater depth.
(3) Time to allow for the exploration and testing of alternative methods of working and for closer involvement in the black communities.

**Training Unit and Student Placements**
7.17    Approximately one hundred students from CQSW courses have a practical work placement in WMCPACS each year. Most students are supervised in their placement by individual probation officers and a small number have their placements in the two Home Office funded training units based at Newton Street, Birmingham and Bankfield House, Wolverhampton where groups of students are supervised by SPOS. Both units draw cases for students from areas where a cross-section of multi-cultural work is possible, and students are therefore in a position to gain practical experience under supervision.

7.18    This is obviously not so for all students on placement in West Midlands County Probation and After-Care Service, as fieldwork supervisors are widely dispersed throughout the areas.

7.19    Many students and new officers have commented on lack of cultural information on CQSW courses – the little offered being in 'optional extras', thus not chosen by those who lack interest. Two students on placement in multi-racial areas quickly recognised their deficiencies and requested ethnic studies on their courses when given open options.

7.20    As an illustration of the need for education for working with black people during training the Adviser learned from one new officer that he received ten cases relating to West Indians/Africans on taking up his appointment.

7.21  One Training Unit SPO had engaged in social work abroad and is aware of the need to introduce students to the cultural dimensions of their work. He does this by linking with community resources in addition to casework and enquiries.

7.22  Agreement has been reached in respect of the other unit that the Ethnic Adviser should convene seminars for student discussion on the cultural implications of their practical work. If this proves fruitful, it may be possible to develop opportunities to link other groups of students on fieldwork placement to participate in seminars related to practice. Also students could be linked into any community culture training as it develops – see 'Training'.

7.23  There is also opportunity for the development of project or research work for students in this area of work.

7.24  Any cultural teaching given on courses needs to be followed through in the field with additional 'nuts and bolts' of probation practice. If it can be introduced at this early stage, new officers may have more to contribute to colleagues and greater confidence in working with clients of various cultural backgrounds.

7.25  Many new officers come to West Midlands County Probation and After-Care Service from the local training courses and therefore it is likely will have experienced probation practice somewhere in West Midlands County Probation and After-Care Service in training. It would seem an investment as well as a wider contribution to training, therefore, to ensure that *all* students have the opportunity for contact with different culture groups during training.

### Recruitment and Deployment of Black officers within Service
7.26  As Probation Service policy is now to employ only trained officers, WMCPACS is dependent upon the output from social work training courses for potential applicants from the ethnic minorities.

7.27  In 1979 the Midlands Region of CCETSW convened a small working group to consider the recruitment to the personal social services of people from ethnic minority groups and other related issues, to consider possible ways forward. The Assistant Chief Probation Officer (Training) has been a corresponding member of that group and their report has been completed.

7.28 Initiatives are therefore being taken to investigate and assist in recruitment and training processes which are being supported by West Midlands County Probation and After-Care Service. The Deputy Chief Probation Officer (Recruitment and Staff Development), has also confirmed the commitment of the Service towards attracting and employing officers from the ethnic minorities.

7.29 During the course of discussions with officers, the following views were expressed:

(1) Recruitment of staff of various ethnic origins would be welcomed by the Service.
(2) It was thought that their all round professional development should be the first consideration of the Service and therefore it was *not* the expectation that such officers would necessarily involve themselves proportionately more with ethnic minorities than their colleagues.
(3) Flexibility was also considered to be important and it was thought that if a request for specialised involvement is made at any point – either by individual preference or interest, or in response to Service needs – then such situations should be given special consideration. Examples are:
Detached SPO working on Handsworth Project.
PO at Coventry of Asian origin involved with a high number of Asian clients.
(4) Some officers in multi-racial areas felt it would be most beneficial for the Probation Service to be seen by the clients and community as more representative of the ethnic groups within the areas.
(5) Officers with various ethnic backgrounds are often used within the team or office as an internal resource and informal contact with colleagues was thought to be a valuable channel for cultural learning to take place.

7.30 Courses offering professional training for social workers are more likely to accept applicants who have had social work experience through previous employment, such as Probation ancillary workers. Black people have a great deal to offer the Service in this capacity and as members of the Administrative, clerical and typing staff.

7.31 At 30th November 1979 professional and administrative staff of Asian or Afro-Caribbean origins employed by WMPACS is as follows:

S.P.O.1)
P.O.9)  out of total of 372                                        = 3.72%

Probation Assistant – 1 out of a total of 34          = 2.94%

Administrative/Clerical
Typing staff – 8 out of a total of 171                    = 4.67%

**Interpreters**

7.32  An assessment of language-comprehension needed to cope with varying situations is an important aspect of communication. Such assessments have to be made by officers interviewing a person in *any* group where there *may* be evidence of communication/comprehension difficulties, ie, physical and mental handicap, the deaf, children and elderly.

7.33  It is difficult to quantify 'adequate' English as the command of language needed to meet specific situations differs. The level required to perform certain tasks such as shopping is different from that needed to explain symptoms of illness or to cope in situations heightened by conflict, crisis and anxiety.

7.34  One of the first tasks of an officer is to assess whether his contact is able to comprehend fully the material he needs to convey and is able to respond and enter into discussion as appropriate.

7.35  One example is that of the Court Duty Officer. He collates basic information, and his assessment of the subject's level of English is often given in writing to the officer who has to prepare the Social Enquiry Report when a far greater level of language comprehension will be necessary. At this stage fluent communication between the parties is essential. Errors can be perpetuated many times over as a person moves through the system. It is therefore of paramount importance to give consideration to the use of an interpreter, whom to use and the way the interview is to be undertaken.

7.36  Such assessments take place at pre-determined stages and further re-evaluation of communication needs are necessary according to the task, which may also include members of the subject's family, particularly if he is a juvenile, or if he is taken into custody and discussion with other members of the household is necessary. Assessment is also important in terms of supervision of Probation and other statutory order as such arrangements may be long term.

7.37  Non-English speaking people are already at a disadvantage within the judicial system which can be alleviated by the use of communication skills and attention to evaluation of language comprehension and the development of efficient methods of communication.

**Methods used in the Probation Service:**

7.38　A wide variety of methods are used by officers to obtain information when there are language difficulties.

(a) Use of contact's family members as interpreters, including children.

(b) Use of interpreter provided by the family who may be a relative, friend or neighbour. (*Interpreters provided by families often do not speak English well enough for exact translation*).

(c) Use by contact or his family of self-styled adviser/interpreter who charges the family for his services.
Often advice is given on what to say and information is given to create a good impression. It has been known for such persons to take payments to 'secure an acquittal'.

(d) Use of a Voluntary Associate as part of his/her voluntary service.

(e) Use of official bodies, such as Community Relations Councils, International Social Services.

(f) Use of community resources:
Examples given: Asian Resource Centre;
Lane Neighbourhood Centre;
Sparkhill Education Centre;
Schools which are also Community Centres;

(g) Use of paid interpreters provided by BIT (Birmingham Interpreting and Translating Agency).

(h) Use of any person proficient in language required, paid Probation Service rates.

(i) Use of religious/community leaders.

7.39　Improvements in our methods of communication could be brought about by:

Improvement in skills of assessment of language – comprehension needed to engage in a variety of tasks.

Awareness of the need to extend the range of enquiries beyond the contact as appropriate to the situation.

Working towards elimination from reports of comments or implications that officers were unable to communicate with the contact or those closely involved in enquiries, either clearly or comprehensively or in some recorded instances, at all.

Recognition that interviewing through a third person is a difficult operation and is a skill to be developed which could usefully be built into Communication Skills courses.

Some officers are of the opinion that having chosen to reside here the responsibility lies with the contact to establish his methods of communication or to accept the resulting disadvantages of non-communication. It is *unquestionably* our responsibility to provide the court with information required and therefore it follows that it is our responsibility to enable the contact to give it.

Numerous suggestions have been received requesting a 'Central Register of Interpreters'. Such a register it is hoped would provide interpreters who:

(a) are conversant with the nature of our work.

(b) Have been recommended and their interpretative skills tested.

(c) As part of their task they would be encouraged to give cultural interpretations of the material as appropriate and who would add his or her own perceptions of the situation if invited to do so. This, it is suggested, would provide a wider perception and a learning experience for officers who require it.

The register would record skills in various languages, availability and suitability for particular tasks.

7.40   It is recognised, however, that it is important for officers to develop and use their own contacts thus establishing a working relationship when possible.

7.41   The Probation Service is not responsible for provision of interpreters in Court. It is the responsibility of the prosecution to make provision for interpreters although occasionally informal use is made of friends or relatives accompanying the defendant. Provision for payment is made by the Court.

7.42   In Evidence and Recommendations to the Royal Commission on Criminal Procedure by CRE[1] attention is drawn to a number of areas of concern for non-English speaking defendants including:

(1) that interpreters supplied by the prosecution regard themselves as 'police interpreters' and may be reluctant to help a defendant communicate with his own lawyer. Even if he does so he may not be trusted by the defendant to interpret impartially.

---

[1]CRE Publication November 1978.

(2) that the standard of translation offered by non-professional interpreters (ie, friends or relatives) is often low and on occasions advice is being
offered by the interpreter.

7.43  Recommendation was made that interpreters should be recruited by the
Magistrate's Courts and a list of 'approved' interpreters should be made
available to prosecution and defence alike.[2]

7.44  Probation Officers have reservations in respect of the interpreting provision made in Courts at the present time and arrangements are sometimes
made for volunteers to accompany a non-English speaking defendent to
Court to ensure that proceedings are understood and clear translation is
given.

**Use of Probation Volunteers**

7.45  The exact number of black volunteers currently engaged in volunteer work
for West Midlands County Probation and After-Care Service has not yet
been determined. The numbers are probably very small indeed in relation
to the amount of contact taking place between Officers and black people
which includes work at the Social Enquiry Report stage not quantified in
this report.

7.46  In the areas where a few Officers are committed to the use of black
volunteers they praise their efforts highly, close working relationships
develop and cultural learning takes place rapidly.

7.47  Illustrations of use of volunteers include:

(1) Accompanying officers as interpreter/adviser on enquiries.
(2) Assessing family need following custodial sentence.
(3) Visiting families to discuss 'cases' with parents or elders and joining in
the male group with understanding of procedure and rituals for the
male group view of a situation – often an important aspect within the
Asian culture.
(4) Advising on a range of practical matters pertaining to 'the system'.
(5) Visiting prisoners, particularly when the prisoner does not speak
English, to relieve isolation.
(6) Transport, escort and interpreter service for Asian ladies needed when
visiting prisons, DHSS, doctors and hospitals, schools, etc.
(7) Supervising all types of orders (in consultation with Supervising

---

[2]Recommendation No. 14.

Officer) particularly when no English is spoken, including arranging and overseeing supervised access to children.

7.48 Some Officers have identified youth clubs, community centres or other organisations which, in offering individual or group involvement on a voluntary basis, have proved beneficial to users of the Probation Service and in many instances have been particularly helpful in assisting numbers of black groups.

7.49 There are issues relating to the use of black volunteers needing further exploration and debate. During discussion with Officers, the basic assumption was made that black volunteers would be expected to be used in tasks pertaining to people with the same ethnic background. The black volunteers main value is seen in understanding the cultural background, language, family dynamics, attitudes etc, of people of his own ethnic origins. Such an assumption would preclude a black volunteer from gaining cross-cultural social work experience which would be particularly valuable assets if he is considering applying for professional social work training.

7.50 Questions have been raised regarding the position of volunteers who offer interpreting skills as part of their voluntary service and whether this constitutes exploitation by accepting a free service for which payment is available. It is thought by management that this is quite acceptable if it has been agreed that it is *this* skill that is being volunteered; however, there may be exceptions when payment is justified.

7.51 Complaint has been made by one black volunteer who was dissatisfied with being continually used only for her interpreting skill, when she had been assured that she would be involved with the users of the Probation Service in a variety of tasks.

7.52 There are officers who are committed to working with volunteers who admit to certain reservations in the recruitment and use of black volunteers:

(a) They presume, frequently without any evidence that volunteers from ethnic minorities will inevitably press their cultural views on the client;
(b) they are anxious that they will not be able to understand what a volunteer is doing if he is allowed to work within his own cultural system, and officers will thus lose control.
(c) they have reservations about the volunteer accepting the code of confidentiality.

(d) They are worried about the possibilities of mis-matching volunteer and client and thus worsening the client's situation (the difficuties which arose from a West Indian client being introduced to a volunteer from a different Caribbean island are cited).

(e) they lack confidence in the recognition such volunteers give to the importance of written records of contacts with clients, and even their ability to provide them.

7.53    It is probably that the idea of offering voluntary service in the community by attachment to a statutory agency will be new to many black people. They are unikely to know how to volunteer their services or what such a role would entail. By developing a policy clarifying some of these issues and by providing adequate preparatory training courses for black volunteers WMCPACS would considerably expand the pool of cultural expertise available within the service, as well as forging closer links with black communities and groups. The imaginative use of black volunteers is one key to ensuring that communication takes place between different ethnic groups, and may be one of the few ways in which the service can adequately attempt to meet the needs of black clients.

# 8.   Development of Future Resources

## Information Service

8.1    The central provision of cultural information is being developed as a resource for Officers which will include:

(1) Basic cultural information in the form of Educational Packs and individual fact and information sheets.
(2) Collection and tabulation of articles and papers including extracts from Social Work Journals.
(3) Ethnic Section of the Lending Library.
(4) Statistical Data and Research Material.
(5) Register of Interpreters and Translators.
(6) Register of recommended films.
(7) Video tapes, maps and display material for training purposes.
(8) Information relating to current Legislation.
(9) Hostel provision relating to special accommodation for Ethnic Minority Groups.
(10) International links with contacts for enquiries abroad.
(11) Location of community information services and specialised information offered, eg, Immigrants Advisory Services, Law Centres, Community Relations Councils.

## Consultancy Service

8.2    A number of requests have been received from individual officers supported by their SPOs for a consultancy service and they query whether the Adviser's post already covers such a service.

8.3    Points made during disussion include:
(a) Some SPOs have expressed feelings of inadequacy in offering new or less experienced officers the depth of supervision, practical information or advice required in cases where the assessment of the cultural factors are an important consideration. These Senior Officers feel that they would advice their officers to consult in certain circumstances if such a service is available.
(b) Particular concern exists in relation to recommendations in the Divorce

and Domestic Courts in respect of custody and access reports. The prime area of concern is the consideration of the Asian cultural implications to be taken into account but also there have been cases with West Indian background of equal complexity. It is important for the Probation Service to be able to give accurate advice on cultural matters.

In one instance a case was adjourned for the probation officer to take further advice regarding the cultural accuracy of his recommendation, which was quite correct but had been challenged by the solicitor involved.

(c) In areas where officers rarely come in contact with black people, possibly little experience exists to deal with the unusual or unexpected case that may involve complex cultural factors.

8.4    It is suggested there is sufficient need, as illustrated, to recommend a Consultancy Service should be made available to the County, which was not explicit in the original job specification of the Ethnic Adviser.

**Research/Data Collection**

8.5    Within WMCPACS a number of people at all levels including students have undertaken research projects during the past few years, either within groups or as individuals. It has been a difficult decision whether to present any samples of these projects and the decision not to do so has been made because some of this work is unfinished and there is no reliable record of all that has been done. Such data collected varies widely in presentation, in content, size of samples, methods of collection, and the inferences drawn from it.

8.6    During January to July 1979, in Birmingham City Magistrates' Courts, data was collected relating to the 2,405 males and 338 females aged between 17 and 21 years who appeared during that period. Information extracted can be broken down into basic ethnic groups.

8.7    This was a conjoint exercise by the Home Office Inspectorate and West Midlands County Probation and After-Care Service and the collection of data was undertaken by STEP personnel employed for that purpose. Discussions are currently taking place regarding evaluation and potential use of this data which is the property of West Midlands Probation and After-Care Service, which will be most valuable in helping to evaluate our smaller pieces of research.

8.8    Research, particularly in the ethnic field is one of the most controversial and delicate issues in West Midlands County Probation and After-Care

Service at the present time. This subject has been of particular interest to officers in group discussion. Criticisms have been voiced and constructive comment given is summarised as follows:

(1) The Service needs to develop a more professional and organised approach to research and data collection.
(2) Co-operation of all interested parties should be sought before research takes place.
(3) Comprehensive samples are advised. There has been criticism of surveys which are:
   (a) Too small in numbers which distort the sample when converted to percentages.
   (b) Too narrow in focus that they exclude important relevant factors.
   (c) Are taken over a short period of time, not allowing for seasonal and other variations.
(4) Comparative samples are advised, ie, similar data to be collected in different courts, offices or areas.
(5) Additional evaluation by an impartial assessor is suggested.
(6) Clarification of the purpose of the research is suggested as important, with information regarding intended readership.
(7) A few individual officers are opposed to collection of statistical data.
   (a) of any kind
   (b) particularly related to ethnic minorities.

8.9 Officers receive impressions of trends and social changes from a variety of sources and are able to give pointers to areas where data at an early stage could provide a basis for action or consideration of policy/practice. The ethnic field is only one section of a spectrum where these impressions apply.

8.10 The data presented in the statistical section of this report confirms current concerns expressed by officers and identifies the need for further exploration of all the possible causal factors involved which may account for the statistically significant differences observed.

8.11 For instance a high priority must be given to the figures in TABLE 5 which show that compared to the white group ALL black groups were more likely, proportionately, to be subject to supervision on Licence, reflecting the comparatively high numbers of young black people serving custodial sentences.

8.12 The complexity of exploring the possible causal factors involved must be recognised and the following is given as an example of the inadvisability of drawing immediate conclusions from statistics alone.

8.13    Contributory factors which might be explored in relation to interpretation of the Detention Centre and Borstal figures presented in TABLE 5 might include:

(a) the age distribution in the population.
(b) the nature/severity of the offence. (Recent evidence from a Birmingham court survey shows that black people are over represented in certain categories of offence and under represented in others).
(c) previous convictions (if any) including nature of offence and sentence imposed.
(d) previous opportunity for supervision in the community.
(e) quality, effectiveness, methods used and length of order of previous contact with Probation Service.
(f) opportunity afforded the defendent for legal assistance.
(g) plea entered.
(h) whether plea was subsequently changed.
(i) whether any change of plea was directly related to lowering of charges
(j) whether committed to the Crown Court for sentence.
(k) whether defendent opted for trial at Crown Court. (Recent survey shows proportionately more black people are sentenced in Crown Courts.)
(l) whether a Social Enquiry Report was available/requested.
(m) recommendations made in SER.
(n) whether recommendations were followed.
(o) quality and nature of content of SER.
(p) whether defendent was unemployed at the time of sentencing (therefore may be less likely to receive a fine).
(q) whether the defendent was of 'no fixed abode' or had accommodation problems.
(r) whether communication difficulties have been identified.
(s) whether there are differences between white and black groups relating to early discharge of licences.
(t) any other recurring factors.

8.14    In exploring the above, information may be discovered which could also be related to other observable differences.

8.15    The appointment in early 1980 of a Research/Information Officer acknowledges the large task awaiting attention in relation to Research in Probation in which ethnic field should take a high priority.

# 9.    Conclusions and The Way Forward

9.1    The conclusions which are drawn from this study can be summarised as follows:

9.2    Reviews which determine current policy and practice of agencies in relation to services offered to ethnic minority groups are of value. They assist in:

(a) Monitoring service provision, the quality of service offered and the manner in which it is delivered.
(b) Providing a base from which changes in policy and practice can be considered/implemented.
(c) Determining aspects of work which need further investigation or continued monitoring.
(d) Giving indications as to whether racial prejudice or other factors cause discriminatory practices to operate either directly or indirectly.

9.3    The collection of statistical data is relevant and useful as it can quickly establish:

(a) The ethnic minority groups most in need of the agencies' service.
(b) The location of ethnic minority groups (areas of settlement in relation to client need).
(c) The nature of contact with the agency.
(d) Identification of statistically significant differences which may be occurring between ethnic minority groups and the majority (ie, white) group.

9.4    This report established:

(a) The ethnic minority groups in need of support are West Indians and, to a lesser extent, Asians (people from the sub-continent of India).
(b) The concentration of the black communities is centred on the older inner-city areas and therefore a high percentage of black people are living in areas with compound environmental problems and are ex-

periencing social and economic deprivation. The percentage of black clients is highest in these areas.

(c) The highest proportion of black clients in contact with the Probation Service are juveniles and young persons. A high percentage of work undertaken with the young black offender is during or following custodial sentences.

(d) A number of areas where statistically significant differences are observed in the proportion of ethnic groups represented under different categories of supervision.

9.5    In view of the general inadequacy of cross-cultural social work pre-service training it is vital that agencies should pay attention to in-service training opportunities and develop their own programmes specifically related to the aims and the tasks of the agency.

9.6    The provision of equal opportunities for all ethnic minorities requires working towards winning general approval and acceptance of positive discrimination as a means of offering compensatory support to meet special needs.

9.7    It is advisable to develop a variety of projects accepting that there will be risks in doing so in order that a number of approaches can be evaluated and compared to assess the way forward in the future.

9.8    In order to develop a professional service to the ethnic minority groups a high level of personal evaluation of work is essential.

9.9    There is urgent need for sharing information, knowledge and understanding of cross-cultural social work within the Probation Service both locally and nationally, in linking with other agencies to learn from them and with them and to become closely involved with the black communities in order to share our understanding of each other, relating that understanding to the services offered.

**The Way Forward**

9.10    Time has passed since the compilation of this report and while awaiting its publication WMCPACS has moved forward. All the recommendations are being followed. An information and consultancy service now operates and is being used increasingly by the Service, students and others outside the Service.

9.11    Training programes are expanding rapidly, with the Service designing and organising its own cultural courses and all courses developed by WMCPACS are now considered for the inclusion of a cultural dimension related to the course content.

9.12   A programme has been devised offering all students on placements with WMCPACS the opportunity of cultural experiences presented in a variety of ways, most of which are organised by ethnic minority groups within their own communities.

9.13   There are cultural interest groups forming amongst officers in some areas and special groups are considering issues which have not been approached before. The Midlands Regional Divorce Court Welfare Officers Group are considering aspects of cross-cultural domestic work. The Volunteers Working Party and Volunteers Co-ordinators Groups have met to consider issues relating to recruitment of black volunteers and the Administrative Officers Standing Group are giving consideration to matters relating to administrative, clerical and typing staff.

9.14   The Ethnic Minorities Liaison Advisory Group has a full agenda and has been considering areas for further research including Social Enquiry Reports with particular reference to black people. The group will be examining the implications of the proposed British Nationality Bill.

9.15   An exciting development is the recent decision by management to support the distribution of an Ethnic Minorities Information Bulletin three times per year which will be distributed within WMCPACS but will also be available outside the Service and it is hoped that this will develop into an inter-service communication channel. In addition to information and initiatives relating to WMCPACS, the black communities, other Services and agencies will be invited to contribute thus developing a better understanding of the cultural aspects of our work.

9.16   The Cultural Resource Centre is beginning to play its part in providing a focal point for black youth and those interested in meeting with them. Handsworth Alternatives Scheme is just about to take over adjoining premises thus physically linking these two major resources.

9.17   The Day Activity Centre is fully operational with a multi-racial clientele and has expanded its sphere of activities to include driving simulators on which driving instruction is given and the car repair and engineering workshop is open. These facilities will shortly be linked to a number of motor projects which are being promoted in various part of the County, ie,

Coventry, Wolverhampton, Dudley and Birmingham. All schemes are community based and are run in partnership with the Probation Service and the community: there is evidence that approximately 25% of Borstal trainees in West Midlands neighbourhood Borstal have been sentenced for taking and driving away motor vehicles. These schemes take West Midlands into the field of 'auto-crime prevention' and it is hoped young people's interest in motor vehicles will be chanelled constructively by learning to drive, repair and customise cars. Land has been acquired for the Birmingham project to develop a motor-adventure track and a multi-purpose complex which will offer facilities for banger racing, motor cycle and go-cart racing, with areas forming their own teams and using the track as a central provision. It is stressed that this is a provision which will be open to offenders and non-offenders and it may also be opened up for schools so that it will not be viewed as a reward for crime. There will be opportunities for black youths to participate fully, and to learn and compete on an equal footing.

9.18 Two other action projects are under consideration, both of which are likely to be specifically for black offenders and it is hoped they will be developed by the communities themselves.

9.19 It is hoped that officers will increasingly recognise the value of utilising community resources and that they will actively participate in encouraging individuals and groups of the ethnic minority communities to develop supportive ventures for offenders, thus, the existing expertise and goodwill can be linked through the Service to the offender, who will then have the benefit of community support in addition to that offered by the individual officer. There are growing indications, particularly within the Asian communities that community support, advice and practical assistance can be organised for both offenders and their families.

9.20 A declared intention for the Service as a whole, outlined in the Chief Probation Officer's recent paper 'The Next Five Years' is 'to divert from custody or residential care as many as possible of those who do not require that expensive provision. There is evidence that the younger age group find their way into custody or care and that this reinforces their chances of recidivism. To this end the priorities of the Service must be:

(1) Effective involvement in the process of sentencing. Recommending non-custodial penalties for some of those now sent to prison department establishments or committed to care.

(2) Managing community provisions which hold the confidence of courts and public.'

9.21  We believe the black communities will be prepared to support us in these objectives in the recognition that their young people are frequently being sentenced to detention centre and borstal training and will work with us in the provision of realistic alternatives to custodial sentences.

9.22  The social and economic position of an individual within Society, how he is viewed by the community, the provisions made for his welfare and the opportunities afforded to him to improve his position, are matters of importance to those such as Probation Officers who become involved in seeking out and helping to relieve aspects of deprivation and discomfort affecting people's lives.

9.23  In areas where stress is evident and resources are strained to their limits it is all too often the case that black people are identified as the cause of, or at least as contributing towards, the social problems of the community as a whole. Scant recognition is given to the positive elements of their settlement in this County, many of which have been pointed out by officers working in close contact with black people. A richness has been added to local cultures through music, language, religion, arts and crafts and their contributions in work, business enterprise and sport, and an example provided in the closeness and responsibilities family and kin share.

9.24  The rewards to be gained by those willing to invest in cross-cultural relationships are great. They offer a new dimension to our preception of ways of living and by acknowledging our differences and sharing them together we learn to see our Western culture more clearly with all its imperfections and ourselves as its product. Positive attributes of other cultures are then more readily identified and assistance can be given to those who seek only to retain or to reshape their cultural identity and to live in dignity and self respect within a society which is now also their own. The potential rewards for a multi-racial community are great if the black members are assisted in raising their social and economic position.

9.25  It would be remiss not to mention the wide range of views expressed by officers who have challenged the validity of the creation of this post. Many feel the pressure of work is heaviest in the field where there is the direct personal contact with the offender and that any additional staffing resources should be deployed in the highly multi-racial areas. There is the belief that one person can have little impact in a county this size with diverse ethnic minority groups and suspicion exists that this post was created in order to pay lip service to the subject and that the task of the Ethnic Adviser would be to 'keep the lids in place'.

9.26   A few officers feel that a specialist unit would provide a more efficient and effective service. There are also those who, although clearly condemning racism, find it difficult, even impossible, to accept positive discrimination as a form of compensatory support. They feel the Service is openly supporting a separatist policy which will not assist in integration.

9.27   Lids are being lifted and perhaps this report will provide another perspective for further thought on views expressed which are undoubtedly reflected in the wider society and upon those which may be of even greater importance as yet left unvoiced.

9.28   This multiplicity of viewpoints means that changes in policy and practice often call for changes in attitudes and beliefs which have been held for a lifetime. It is an uneasy path to tread as this subject raises both the emotions and the defences. Ultimately the extent of progress and change rests with every individual. It is the responsibility of every individual within WMCPACS to ensure that those of all races who, regrettably, share our problems and our prisons are offered every opportunity to improve the quality of their lives and that justice is tempered with understanding.

# 10. Recommendations of West Midlands County Probation and After-Care Service

10.1    On 14th February 1980 this report was presented to Management of the West Midlands County Probation & After-Care Service who accepted all the recommendations and designated responsibility for their implementation within the County Service.

### Social Policy
10.2    That the Service should be prepared to consider in what ways it can influence social policy in relation to black groups.

### Discrimination
10.3    That there should be discussion of any actions or practices which are perceived as direct or indirect discrimination within the Service's operation, in order to ensure delivery of a service under the terms of the Race Relations Act.

10.4    Management needs to consider the way in which the Probation Service should respond in instances of apparent and actual discrimination within institutions and other related agencies and fields and assist staff in learning constructive ways of handling such issues as they arise.

### Linked Projects
10.5    That WMCPACS should encourage appropriate initiatives by officers and other bodies and assist in the development of projects in accordance with community needs.

### Resources
10.6    That there should be examination whether more resources are required in areas where officers are carrying a high volume of work with black people.

### Training
10.7    That all avenues open for training of officers should be explored and new approaches developed in order to attract and interest officers at all levels of development.

10.8    That WMCPACS should ensure it is in a position to contribute towards the cultural dimension of social work training on CQSW and other courses, as appropriate.

10.9    That the Service should ensure multi-cultural experience is available to students on placements in WMCPACS, where possible.

**Recruitment and deployment**

10.10   That WMCPACS should continue to support initiatives undertaken by CCETSW to recruit from all ethnic groups.

10.11   That WMCPACS should reappraise its recruitment and use of volunteers, ancillaries, admin and clerical staff from black groups and ensure that opportunities are available to all people to have pre-professional social work experience.

**Specialist knowledge and experience**

10.12   That officers with expertise in this field should be encouraged to develop their skills to an advanced level and contribute towards training.

**Interpreters**

10.13   That WMCPACS should accept it is a Service responsibility to ensure that communication takes place with all relevant people, at a level which is adequate for the task in hand.

10.14   That relevant communication skills should be given more attention and included in training programmes.

10.15   That local registers of interpreters should be compiled for each area and this information collated into a central register.

10.16   That the interpreter/advisory service should be developed, to include cultural interpretations of information received.

**Volunteers**

10.17   That ways of attracting black volunteers should be explored.

10.18   That officers should be encouraged to use black volunteers as a resource.

10.19   That there should be debate on a range of issues relating to the use of black volunteers.

### Information Service
10.20 That a comprehensive information service should be developed.

### Consultancy Service
10.21 That an ethnic consultancy service should be available to the County.

### Research
10.22 That the compilation and evaluation of research and data available should be seen as a priority in relation to our work with black people. That priorities in relation to future research projects in this field should be considered.

10.23 That officers should be encouraged to take professional advice when entering into the field of research or data collection.

### Social Work Methods
10.24 That Social Work methods should be re-appraised in relation to black people in general but specifically in respect of supervision of the young black offender with the aim of offering an appropriate and effective service which will assist in reducing the number of young black offenders in custody.

### Community
10.25 That WMCPACS should explore ways of publicising the functions of the Probation Service within the black communities. That links should be developed with black communities enabling them to express their views of service delivery and contribute towards an examination of social work methods.

10.26 That the needs of different black groups and communities should be appraised in order to develop appropriate responses.

10.27 That contact should be sought with black self-help groups.

### Linking Nationally
10.28 That WMCPACS should initiate contact with other Services in relation to work in this field.

### Title
10.29 That the title of 'County Adviser to WMCPACS on Ethnic Minorities' be changed to 'Ethnic Adviser to WMCPACS.'

# STATISTICAL SURVEY

# Statistical Survey

1.     'There are a number of general reasons why up-to-date and accurate statistics concerning the position of racial minorities should be collated. First, they are a necessary though not of course a sufficient condition, for rational discussion and understanding of race relations. Second, without knowledge of the existing situation and more particularly of developing trends, there can be no sound basis for the assessment of development of policy. Third, identification of needs, and thus the application of policy, is likely to be arbitrary if not impossible in the absence of good data.'

2.     'Against this it can be argued that the collection of data on a racial basis is itself discriminatory, and emphasises and perpetuates distinctions that might otherwise be ignored. However, when race affects social relations and the application of resources, as it patently does, statistics are an indispensable prerequisite for policies aimed at improving race relations. We do not believe it is better to turn a blind eye'.

Home Office Advisory Committee on
Race Relations Research
(HMSO 1975)

# WMCPACS – A Survey – 30th November 1979

## Aims

3.     The aims of the survey were to discover the EXTENT, LOCATION AND NATURE of the work of WMCPACS in relation to black people.*

## SUMMARY OF FINDINGS

4.     The findings of the survey may be summarised as follows:

(1) The statistical survey showed that 13.9% of clients on West Midland Probation Officers caseloads at 30th Novbember 1979 were from ethnic minority groups. (Table 2).

(2) In addition to the statutory and voluntary supervision of clients a great deal of work with black people, which has not been measured, is also taking place at Social Enquiry Report stage. (Pre-sentencing).

(3) The largest single ethnic minority group in contact with the Probation Service are West Indians who comprise 8.6% of the total county caseload. (Table 2).

(4) Asians (ie, people from the sub-continent of India) collectively form 3% of the total county caseload. (Table 2).

(5) Tests applied to the statistical survey identify a number of statistically significant differences in the proportion of ethnic groups represented under different categories of supervision.

(6) Similar proportions of West Indians/Africans, clients of mixed racial origins/other non-British and the white group were in contact with the Service in the supervision and custody/post custody categories.

(7) Asians were proportionately *under*-represented in the supervision category and *over*-represented in the custody/post custody category. (Table 3).

(8) In the Matrimonial section clients of mixed racial origins/other non-British were *over*-represented in comparison to the white group. (Table 3).

**Supervision Categories**

(9) Probation Orders – Asians and West Indians/Africans were *under*-represented in comparison to the white group. (Table 4).

---

*Classification of ethnic groups – Appendix 5.

(10) C. & Y.P. Supervision Orders – Asians and West Indians/Africans were *over*-represented in comparison to the white group. (Table 4).

(11) Within the 'Supervision' category, ethnic minority clients, particularly Asians, were, when compared to the white group, more likely to be JUVENILES (ie, on C. & Y.P. Supervision) whereas the white group, were more likely to be ADULTS (ie, on Probation Orders) – clients of mixed racial origin/other non-British excluded. (Table 4).

### Supervision on Licence (post custody)

(12) Detention Centre Licences – West Indians/Africans and Asians were *over*-represented in comparison to the white group. (Table 5).

(13) Borstal Licence Supervision – clients of mixed racial origins/other non-British and West Indians/Africans were *over*-represented in comparison to the white group. (Table 5).

(14) Parole/Life Licence – Asians were *over*-represented in comparison to the white group. (Table 5).

(15) Licences (combined) – All ethnic minority groups were proportionately more likely to be subject to supervision on Licence (ie, following a custodial sentence) than the white group. (Table 5).

(16) Pre-release (during custody) – All ethnic minority groups were *UNDER*-represented in relation to the white group.

(17) Voluntary After-Care (post custody) – West Indians/Africans were *OVER*-represented in comparison to the white group. (Table 5).

(18) Every sub-area in the County is responsible for the supervision of black clients, proportions ranging from 26.5% of Birmingham North's caseload to 6.7% of Walsall/West Bromwich caseload. (Table 6).


## Method

5.   The standard form completed monthly by Administrative officers, quantifying work undertaken by officers and sub-divided into various categories, was adapted to provide the *same* information in relation to black ethnic groups only.

6.   In this way it was possible to compare the survey results with total workload figures.

7.   This form was designed to show the natural division of work between

(1) Supervisory contact as a result of court orders, ie:

Probation Orders
Children and Young Person Supn. Orders
Money Payment Supn. Orders
Matrimonial & Wardship Supn. Orders
Suspended Sentence Supn. Orders
Community Service Orders

(2) Contact as a result of a custodial sentence, ie:

Detention Centre Licence Supn.
Borstal Licence Supervision
Prison Licence Supn.
Voluntary After-Care
Parole Licence Supn.
Pre-release contact (ie, contact with persons in any form of custodial institution currently serving a sentence)
Kindred Social Work (ie, Voluntary assistance by request) is also quantified.

Details of sentencing options showing Probation responsibilities under respective orders – Appendix 3.

8. The prepared forms were distributed, one to each officer currently undertaking any form of client supervision and also to Community Service Units.

9. It was requested that forms were completed to show caseload figures as at 30 November 1979. The response rate was 98% – only 6 out of a total of 300 officers declined to participate. There may, therefore, be fractionally higher numbers of black clients than presented in the results but this is unlikely to represent a significant bias.

## Limitations

10. None of the work undertaken at Social Enquiry Report stage is included in this survey, this is indeed worthy of a separate study.

11. In 1979 WMCPACS prepared over 12,500 reports. Therefore, in *addition* to the statistics presented in this section there is a volume of work with black people *prior to sentencing* that is not quantified.

12. This is the *first* survey of this nature undertaken by WMCPACS. Therefore there is, as yet no comparative material available to show trends.

13. *Although patterns emerge from the statistics which invite speculation, the statistics do not themselves enable any conclusions to be drawn about the reasons for differences in the proportion of black people in each category, such differences are likely to be associated with a number of factors, some specific to each area. It must also be remembered that the clients with whom the service works are determined by the courts, rather than by the service alone, although the importance of Social Enquiry Reports prepared by Officers must not be underplayed. Further research is required both by WMCPACS and other bodies before an analysis of causal factors could be attempted. Such research would need to include policing and sentencing policies as they relate to race.*[1]

[1]See Chapter 8, Development of Future Resources (Research, Data Collection, Statistical Survey, Areas for further exploration).

## Statistical Significance

14. Where there are statistically significant differences in the proportion of each ethnic group in the categories displayed in the following tables, the probability 'expressed as "p"' of the observed difference occurring by chance is given in parenthesis. Throughout this section expressions such as 'more likely', 'less likely', 'over-represented', and 'significantly different' imply statistical significance of at least the 1% level.

## TABLE 2

**Comparison of the Number and Proportion of Each Ethnic Group on WMCPACS Caseload as at 30th November 1979**

| Ethnic Group | Number of Cases | % of Total Caseload | |
|---|---|---|---|
| West indian | 877 | 8.6% | 8.8% |
| African | 16 | 0.2% | |
| Indian | 161 | 1.6% | |
| Pakistani | 122 | 1.2% | 3.0% |
| Afro/Asian | 22 | 0.2% | |
| Mixed Racial Origins | 150 | 1.5% | 2.1% |
| Other non-British | 62 | 0.6% | |
| Total [All Ethnic Minority Groups] | 1,410 | 13.9% | |
| White | 8,691 | 86.1% | |
| **GRAND TOTAL** | **10,101** | **100.0%** | |

## TABLE 2

15. **Comment**

(1) Ethnic Minority groups form 13.9% of WMCPACS caseload.
(2) West Indians form the largest ethnic minority group on caseload –
8.6%.
(3) Asian groups collectively form only 3% of caseload.
(4) There are almost as many people of mixed racial origins on caseload as
there are in the largest single Asian group.
(5) No ethnic group emerged in any significant numbers in the 'other
non-British' section.

**Note:** Without reliable census data it has not been possible to show the extent to which
minorities are over (or under) represented on the caseload of WMCPACS in relation to
population.

## TABLE 3

**Comparison of the Number and Proportion of Ethnic Groups
on WMCPACS Caseload According to Category of Supervision**

| Category of Supervision | West Indian/ African | Asian | Mixed Race/ other Non-British | White |
|---|---|---|---|---|
| Supervision[1] | 351 (39.5%) | 84 (27.5%) | 75 (35.4%) | 3,520 (40.5%) |
| Custody/Post Custody[2] | 381 (42.5%) | 175 (57.4%) | 85 (40.1%) | 3,578 (41.2%) |
| Matrimonial and Wardship | 143 (16.0%) | 40 (13.1%) | 49 (23.1%) | 1,275 (14.7%) |
| Kindred Social Work | 18  (2.0%) | 6  (2.0%) | 3  (1.4%) | 318  (3.7%) |
| **TOTAL** | **893 (100.0%)** | **305 (100.0%)** | **212 (100.0%)** | **8,691 (100.0%)** |

1. Supervision       = Probation; Children and Young Persons Act Supervision;
Suspended Sentence Supervision; Money Payment Supervision
and Community Service Orders.

2. Custody/Post Custody = All persons serving sentences who are in contact with the
Probation Service/Detention Centre Licence; Borstal Licence;
Prison Licence; Parole; Life Licence; Voluntary After Care.

**TABLE 3**

16. **Comment**

1. The Two main categories of work on WMCPACS caseload are:
   (a) Various forms of supervision
   (b) Contact during and after custodial sentences
2. At the time this data was collected these two categories each formed approximately 40% of the work of the Service.[1]
3. Ethnic groups (including the 'white' group) were represented in similar proportions in each of the above two categories with the exception that a *greater* proportion of Asians (57.4%) were in the custody/post custody category and a *smaller* proportion (27.5%) were under other forms of supervision.

   [These differences are statistically significant (p = <0.0001)]

4. Similar percentages (approx. 15%) of all ethnic groups appear in the Matrimonial Section with the exception that Mixed Race/other non-British clients were over-represented. (p = <0.01). Of the 49 clients in this group, 40 were children of mixed racial parentage.
5. Small differences in the proportion of each ethnic group utilising the Kindred Social Work Service are not statistically significant.


**TABLE 4**

**Comparison of the Number and Proportion of Ethnic Groups on WMCPACS Caseload According to 'Supervision' Sub-Categories**

| Category of Supervision | West Indian/ African | Asian | Mixed Race/ other Non-British | White |
|---|---|---|---|---|
| Probation | 156 (44.4%) | 26 (31.0%) | 40 (53.3%) | 1,911 (54.3%) |
| C. & Y.P. Supn. | 136 (38.8%) | 44 (52.4%) | 25 (33.3%) | 917 (26.0%) |
| Suspended Sentence Supn. | 8 (2.3%) | 2 (2.4%) | 1 (1.3%) | 160 (4.5%) |
| Money Payment Supn. | 5 (1.4%) | –(– –) | –(– –) | 45 (1.3%) |
| Community Service | 46 (13.1%) | 12 (14.2%) | 9 (12.0%) | 487 (13.8%) |
| **TOTAL** | **351 (100.0%)** | **84 (100.0%)** | **75 (100.0%)** | **3,520 (100.0%)** |

Ref. 1. Tables 4 and 5 sub-divide these two main categories.

**TABLE 4**

17.  **Comment**

1.  **Demographic Patterns**

    In examining figures of the proportion of cases which relate to different age groups, the different demographic structures of different ethnic groups must be borne in mind: In 1971 whereas 24% of the total Great Britain population was under 21, this percentage was 41% of the New Commonwealth and Pakistan population and 46% for population from the American Commonwealth (mainly from the West Indies).

    Estimates produced by the Office of Population Censuses and Statistics indicate that the relative proportions of the population per ethnic group under 21 in 1981 is likely to be similar to those in 1971. These demographic patterns are spelt out in the Appendix to the CRE publication 'Youth in Multi-Racial Society'[1].

2.  **Probation** (ie, Supervision of adults)

    In comparison to the white group where 54.3% of all those under supervision were on Probation:

    (a) Asians were under-represented with 31% on Probation.

    (b) West Indians/Africans were under-represented with 44% on Probation

    [These differences are statistically significant
    $p = <0.001$ and $p = <0.01$ respectively]

    (c) The proportion of mixed race/other non-British on Probation was similar to the white group at 53.3%.

3.  **Children and Young Persons Supervision** (ie, supervision of juveniles)

    The differences between each group with regard to the proportion on Probation are balanced by the differences in the proportion on C. & Y.P. Supervision.

    In comparison to the white group where 26% of those under supervision were on C. & Y.P. Supervision Orders

    (a) Asians were over-represented with 52.4% on C. & Y.P. Supervision

---

[1]Youth in Multi-Racial Society – The Urgent Need for New Policies ('The Fire Next Time'). CRE, 1980.

(b) West Indians/Africans were over-represented with 38.8% on C. & Y.P. Supervision
   [These differences are statistically significant
      p = <0.001]
   From points 1 and 2 above it can be concluded that a greater proportion of West Indians/Africans and particularly Asians under supervision were JUVENILES compared to the white group.

4. **Suspended Sentence Supervision**
   Minimal use is made of this form of supervision with only 11 Suspended Sentence Supervision orders in force for ethnic minorities within the County although with the exception of mixed race/other non-British, this number is not significantly different from the proportion of the white group under this form of supervision.

5. **Money Payment Supervision Orders**
   Minimal use is made of this form of supervision for both white and West Indian/African groups. It is not in use at all for Asian/Mixed Race/non-British.

6. **Community Service Orders**
   There was no statistically significant difference in the proportion of each ethnic group on Community Service.


## TABLE 5

**Comparison of the Number and Proportion of Ethnic Groups on WMCPACS Caseload According to 'Custody/Post Custody' Sub-Categories**

| Category of Supervision | West Indian/ African | Asian | Mixed Race/ other Non-British | White |
|---|---|---|---|---|
| Detention Centre Licence | 61 (16.0%) | 27 (15.6%) | 9 (10.9%) | 329  (8.9%) |
| Borstal Licence | 71 (18.6%) | 11  (6.3%) | 19 (22.9%) | 259  (7.0%) |
| Prison Licence | 26  (6.8%) | 11  (6.3%) | 8  (9.6%) | 175  (4.8%) |
| Parole/Life Licence | 30  (7.9%) | 22 (12.6%) | 5  (6.0%) | 155  (4.2%) |
| Voluntary After-Care | 70 (18.4%) | 28 (16.1%) | 13 (15.7%) | 496 (13.5%) |
| Pre-release | 123 (32.3%) | 75 (43.1%) | 29 (34.9%) | 2,267 (61.6%) |
| **TOTAL** | **381 (100%)** | **174 (100%)** | **83 (100%)** | **3,681 (100%)** |

**TABLE 5**

18. **Comment:**

1. **Licences**

   Taking the combined percentages of the four Licence sub-categories (ie, Detention Centre, Borstal, Prison, Parole/Life Licence) for each ethnic group;

   (a) Proportion between each ethnic minority group was similar. (Average 46.5%).

   (b) Compared to the white group all ethnic minority groups were more likely to be subject to supervision on Licence

   Combined percentage of Licence sub-categories white group 24.9%

   Combined percentage of Licence sub-categories ethnic minority groups average 46.5%

   [These differences are statistically significant (p = <0.001)]

2. **Detention Centre Licences**

   In comparison to the white group where 8.9% of all those in the custody/post custody category were on D.C. Licence;

   (a) West Indians/Africans were over-represented with 16% on D.C. Licence

   (b) Asians were over-represented with 15.6% on D.C. Licence

   (c) There was no statistically significant difference between Mixed Race/other non-British and the white group.

   [The proportion of the white group on D.C. Licence was significantly less (p = <0.001) than the proportion of West Indians/Africans and Asians on D.C. Licence but NOT Mixed Race/other non-British.]

3. **Borstal Licence**

   In comparison to the white group where 7.0% of all those in the custody/post custody category were on Borstal Licence;

   (a) Mixed Race/other non-British were over-represented with 22.9% on Borstal Licence

   (b) West Indians/Africans were over-represented with 18.6% on Borstal Licence

   (c) The proportion of Asians on Borstal Licence was similar to the white group.

   [The proportion of the white group on Borstal Licence was significantly less (p = <0.001) than the West Indians/Africans and Mixed Race/other non-British on Borstal Licence – but not Asians.]

[Within the ethnic groups the proportion of West Indians/ Africans on Borstal Licence was significantly greater (p = <0.001) than the proportion of Asians on Borstal Licence but similar to the proportion of Mixed Race/other non-British on Borstal Licence.]

4. **Prison Licence**
There was no significant difference between any group on Prison Licence.

5. **Parole and Life Licence**
   (a) In comparison to the white group where 4.2% were on Parole/Life Licence, Asians were over represented with 12.6% on Parole/Life Licence (p = <0.001)
   (b) Within the ethnic minority groups there was no significant difference.

6. **Voluntary After-Care**
   (a) There was no statistically significant difference in the proportion of Asian, Mixed Race/other non-British and the white group in the Voluntary After-Care category
   (b) West Indians were more likely to appear in this category than the white group (p = <0.01), (ie, 18.4% of West Indians/Africans were in the Voluntary After-Care category compared to 13.5% of the white group).

7. **Pre-release** (all persons serving custodial sentences who are in contact with the Probation Service)
The under-representation of the white group on various forms of Licence compared to the ethnic minority groups is balanced by the over-representation of the white group in the pre-release category. Proportionately more of the white group (61.6%) appear in this category compared to ethnic minority groups (average 36.7%).
[This difference is statistically significant (p = <o.001)]

**N.B.** It is outside the boundaries of this report to determine the exact reasons for these observable differences. It is likely that there are numerous factors to be taken into account:
   **e.g.** The age distribution of the ethnic groups in population.
   The composition of the white prison population (eg, the large numbers serving short sentences not appearing on licence).
   The nature and severity of offences and other factors taken into account when sentencing.

## TABLES 6 (A to D)

## Comparison Between WMCPACS Sub-Areas of the Number and Proportion of Ethnic Groups on Area Caseloads

### A. WOLVERHAMPTON

| Ethnic Group | No. on Area Caseload | % of Total Caseload |
|---|---|---|
| West Indian/African | 108 | 14.44 |
| Asian | 44 | 5.88 |
| Mixed Race/other non-British | 13 | 1.74 |
| **TOTAL** | **165** | **22.06** |
| White | 583 | 77.94 |
| **GRAND TOTAL** | **748** | **100.00%** |

### B. DUDLEY/WARLEY

| Ethnic Group | No. on Area Caseload | % of Total Caseload |
|---|---|---|
| West Indian/African | 61 | 4.99 |
| Asian | 41 | 3.36 |
| Mixed Race/other non-British | 22 | 1.80 |
| **TOTAL** | **124** | **10.15** |
| White | 1,098 | 89.85 |
| **GRAND TOTAL** | **1,222** | **100.00%** |

### C. WALSALL/WEST BROMWICH

| Ethnic Group | No. on Area Caseload | % of Total Caseload |
|---|---|---|
| West Indian/African | 45 | 4.52 |
| Asian | 11 | 1.10 |
| Mixed Race/other non-British | 11 | 1.10 |
| **TOTAL** | **67** | **6.72(6)** |
| White | 929 | 93.37 |
| **GRAND TOTAL** | **996** | **100.00%** |

## D. BIRMINGHAM NORTH

| Ethnic Group | No. on Area Caseload | % of Total Caseload |
|---|---|---|
| West Indian/African | 302 | 20.53 |
| Asian | 51 | 3.47 |
| Mixed Race/other non-British | 37 | 2.51 |
| **TOTAL** | **390** | **26.51** |
| White | 1,081 | 73.49 |
| **GRAND TOTAL** | **1,471** | **100.00%** |

## TABLES 6 (E to H)

## E. BIRMINGHAM WEST

| Ethnic Group | No. on Area Caseload | % of Total Caseload |
|---|---|---|
| West Indian/African | 61 | 4.92 |
| Asian | 13 | 1.05 |
| Mixed Race/other non-British | 18 | 1.45 |
| **TOTAL** | **92** | **7.42(53)** |
| White | 1,147 | 92.57 |
| **GRAND TOTAL** | **1,239** | **100.00%** |

## F. BIRMINGHAM EAST

| Ethnic Group | No. on Area Caseload | % of Total Caseload |
|---|---|---|
| West Indian/African | 115 | 9.27 |
| Asian | 45 | 3.63 |
| Mixed Race/other non-British | 25 | 2.01 |
| **TOTAL** | **185** | **14.91** |
| White | 1,056 | 85.09 |
| **GRAND TOTAL** | **1,241** | **100.00%** |

## G. BIRMINGHAM SOUTH

| Ethnic Group | No. on Area Caseload | % of Total Caseload |
|---|---|---|
| West Indian/African | 124 | 7.89 |
| Asian | 52 | 3.31 |
| Mixed Race/other non-British | 58 | 3.69 |
| **TOTAL** | **234** | **14.89** |
| White | 1,338 | 85.11 |
| **GRAND TOTAL** | **1,572** | **100.00%** |

## H. COVENTRY

| Ethnic Group | No. on Area Caseload | % of Total Caseload |
|---|---|---|
| West Indian/African | 31 | 3.25 |
| Asian | 30 | 3.15 |
| Mixed Race/other non-British | 13 | 1.36 |
| **TOTAL** | **74** | **7.76** |
| White | 879 | 92.24 |
| **GRAND TOTAL** | **953** | **100.00%** |

**TABLE 6 (A – H)**

19. **Comment**

1. The distribution of ethnic minority groups on Probation sub-area caseloads is not uniform through the County.
2. The distribution of ethnic minority groups on caseload shows West Indians and Asians in every Probation sub-area of the County.
3. The greatest proportion of ethnic minority clients were, when the data was collected, on caseloads of officers in Birmingham North, which includes the district of Handsworth (26.5% of their total sub-area caseload) and Wolverhampton (22.1% of the total sub-area caseload).
4. In contrast less than 10% of clients on officers' caseloads in Birmingham West, Walsall/West Bromwich and Coventry were from ethnic minority groups.
5. The sub-areas with the greatest number of West Indians/Africans on

caseload were Birmingham North (20.53% of total caseload) and Wolverhampton (14.44% of total caseload).

6. The highest number of Mixed Race/Other non-British clients appear on Birmingham South caseload (3.69% of total area caseload).

7. Asians appear on sub-area caseloads in similar proportion in Wolverhampton, Dudley/Warley, Birmingham North, Birmingham East, Birmingham South and Coventry (between 3.15% and 5.88% of total sub-area caseloads) and a lower proportion in Walsall and Birmingham West (1.10% and 1.05% respectively).

**N.B.** The division of the County into sub-areas for administration purposes cuts across some of the black communities (eg, Muslim Community is divided by the Probation border between Birmingham South and Birmingham East).

Data is available which sub-divides the 'Asian' category into Indian, Pakistani and Afro/Asian sub-groups. The figures for each sub-group on caseload reflect the areas of settlement:

Predominantly Indian settlement – Walsall, Birmingham North, Coventry, Dudley/Warley.

Predominantly Pakistani settlement – Birmingham South and Birmingham East.

Wolverhampton – mixed settlement.

Further details are given in Local Information and Responses (Section 4).

## TABLE 7

### Number and Proportion of Ethnic Minorities
### Serving Community Service Orders

This table is presented separately as three Community Service Units cover the West Midlands County and the figures are not easily divisible into the eight sub-areas.

| Area | Total Area Caseload | No. & % of Ethnic Minorities |
|------|---------------------|------------------------------|
| Birmingham | 269 | 41 (15.2%) |
| Coventry | 63 | 10 (15.9%) |
| West of County | 222 | 16  (7.2%) |
| **TOTAL** | **554** | **67 (12.1%)** |

20. The Community Service Unit based in Wolverhampton covers the whole of the West of the County. The low percentage of black clients on Community Service Orders (7.2%) in this area must be read in relation to the whole of the West of the County (Wolverhampton, Walsall, Dudley/Warley) which includes large areas with low ethnic minority populations.

# APPENDICES

# Appendix 1

## LEGAL RESPONSIBILITIES UNDER RACE RELATIONS ACT, 1976

The Race Relations Act, 1976, Section 71, places the duty on local authorities to promote good race relations, namely,

'It should be the duty of every local authority to make appropriate arrangements with a view to securing that their various functions are carried out with due regard to the need:

(a) to eliminate unlawful racial discrimination.

(b) to promote equality of opportunity and good relations between persons of different racial groups.'

### Racial Discrimination

The Act defines two kinds of racial discrimination:

1. *Direct racial discrimination* which arises where a person treats another person less favourably on racial grounds[1] than he would treat someone else.

2. *Indirect racial discrimination* consists of treatment which may be described as equal in a formal sense as between different racial groups but discriminatory in its effect on one particular racial group.

The Act allows special provision to be made to meet certain special needs for particular ethnic groups, and *permit certain kinds of positive action.*

Section 35, allows provision to be made for the *special needs of racial groups* in education, training and *welfare.*

---

[1] 'Racial grounds' means any of the following grounds: colour, race, nationality (including citizenship or ethnic or national origins).

Sections 37 and 38 permit the provision of training and encouragement for racial groups to take jobs in which their groups have previously been under-represented.

## Section 20 (1)

### Discrimination in the Provision of Goods, Facilities and Services

The Act makes it unlawful for anyone who is concerned with the provision of goods, facilities or services to the public, to discriminate by refusing, or deliberately omitting to provide them, or as regards their quality, or the manner in which, or the terms on which, he provides them.

WMCPACS therefore asks whether it is satisfied with:

(a) The *provision* of its service to all ethnic groups
(b) The *quality* of its service to all ethnic groups
(c) The *manner* in which its services are provided
(d) The *terms* on which its services are provided.

### The Race Relations Act and The Social Services

Further guidance was given in respect of service delivery in a Working Party Report published by the Association of Directors of Social Services and the Commission for Racial Equality[1] which considered the implications of the Race Relations Act 1976 in relation to the Social Services.

The report stressed the need for special thought to be given by Social Services Departments to their work with ethnic minority groups because of the dimension of need caused by:

(a) Newness.
(b) Cultural differences.
(c) Racial prejudice and discrimination.

The Report recommended:

1. That there is an urgent need to review the work of individual depart-

---

[1]'Multi Racial Britain – The Social Services Response', A Working Party Report. CRE publication July 1978.

ments in relation to minority communities in particular and race relations in general. Departments are advised to examine the relevance of their services for a multi-cultural/racial clientele through a systematic review of their policies on a local basis.

2. In such reviews of existing practices, the involvement of ethnic communities is seen as crucial to the development of effective social services.

3. Specific attention is drawn to the black communities regarding the lack of information about their current needs and welfare provision, and the uncertainties about how best to approach them.

# Appendix 2

## STRUCTURE OF WEST MIDLANDS COUNTY PROBATION AND AFTER-CARE SERVICE

### Deployment of Probation Officer Staff as at 30 November, 1979

1 Chief Probation Officer (CPO)

3 Deputy Chief Probation Officers (DCPO)

10 Assistant Chief Probation Officers (ACPO) –

> 1 to each operational area = 8
> 1 Head Office, with training responsibilities
> 1 responsible for Community Service, Birmingham Courts and Inner City Partnership Schemes

63 Senior Probation Officers –

> 42 engaged with fieldwork teams
> 4 Community Service
> 2 HM Prison, Winson Green
> 2 HO Student Training Units
> 2 Head Office, Training Section
> 1 Head Office, Ethnic Minorities
> 4 Hostels
> 6 seconded on CQSW Courses

289 Probation Officers –

> 247 engaged in fieldwork
> 7 Community Service
> 8 HM Prison, Winson Green
> 1 Hostel
> 26 Seconded on CQSW Courses

6 Seconded Staff –

    2 Day Activity Centres
    1 HO Training Centre, London
    1 Katherine Price Hughes House
    1 Community Project
    1 Brockhill Remand Centre

    **372 TOTAL** (full time equivalent 362½)

**West Midlands County Probation and After-Care Service**

**Location of Probation Offices as at May, 1980** (see map 1)

| **Sub-Area** | | **Probation Office Location** | |
|---|---|---|---|
| **A** | Wolverhampton | **a** | **Wolverhampton** |
| | | **b** | **Bilston** |
| **B** | Dudley/Warley | **c** | **Dudley** |
| | | **d** | **Brierley Hill** |
| | | **e** | **Stourbridge** |
| | | **f** | **Oldbury** |
| | | **g** | **Halesowen** |
| | | **h** | **Smethwick** |
| **C** | Walsall/West Bromwich | **i** | **Walsall** |
| | | **j** | **Aldridge** |
| | | **k** | **Wednesbury** |
| | | **l** | **West Bromwich** |
| **D** | Birmingham North | **m** | **Perry Barr** |
| | | **n** | **Sutton Coldfield** |
| **E** | Birmingham West | **o** | **Kent Street** |
| | | **p** | **Harborne** |
| | | **q** | **Selly Oak** |
| **F** | Birmingham East | **r** | **Newton Street** |
| | | **s** | **Saltley** |
| **G** | Birmingham South | **t** | **Stratford Road** |
| | | **u** | **Kings Heath** |
| | | **v** | **Chelmsley Wood** |
| | | **w** | **Solihull** |
| **H** | Coventry | **x** | **Coventry** |
| | | **H.O.** | **Head Office, Birmingham** |
| | | **H.M.P.** | **HM Prison, Winson Green** |

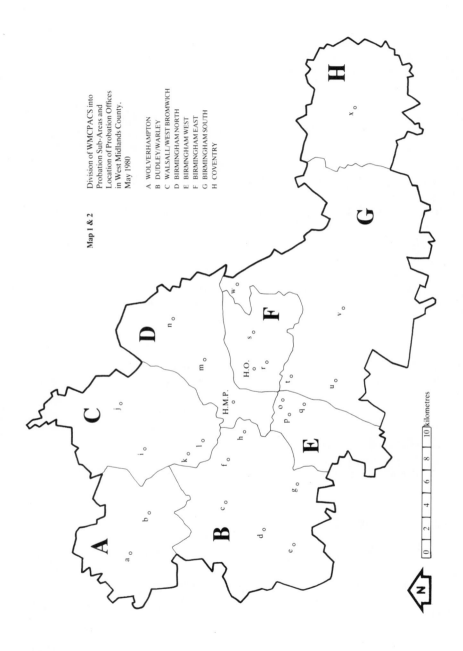

Map 1 & 2

Division of WMCPACS into Probation Sub-Areas and Location of Probation Offices in West Midlands County. May 1980

A WOLVERHAMPTON
B DUDLEY/WARLEY
C WALSALL/WEST BROMWICH
D BIRMINGHAM NORTH
E BIRMINGHAM WEST
F BIRMINGHAM EAST
G BIRMINGHAM SOUTH
H COVENTRY

0 2 4 6 8 10 kilometres

# Appendix 3

## SENTENCING OPTIONS (ADULTS)

### Non-Custodial Treatment
### Absolute Discharge – Any Offence

Where a Court convicts a person of an offence and is of the opinion having regard to the nature of the offence and the character of the offender

(a) that it is inexpedient to inflict punishment
and
(b) a Probation Order is not appropriate
it may make an Order discharging the Defendant.

### Conditional Discharge – Any Offence

The conditions are exactly as above with the addition of two factors:

(1) the order runs for a period not exceeding three years
(2) the Court has a duty to explain to the offender that if he commits another offence during this period he will be liable to be sentenced for the original offence.

### Fine – Any Offence

The maximum fine is laid down by statute. When fixing the amount of the fines the Court takes into account, amongst other things, the means of the offender so far as they appear or are known to the Court.

### Binding Over – Offences involving public disorder

A Bind Over may be used as substitution for punishment but is nearly always used in addition to the normal penalty. The Court fixes the amount, eg, £25 and the duration of the binding over, normally 12 months. If there should be further misconduct the money may be estreated (forfeited).

### Probation Order – Any Offence

Where a person is found guilty of an offence and the Court is of the opinion that, having regard to the circumstances, including the nature of the offence and the character of the offender, it is expedient to do so, the Court may, instead of sentencing him, place him under the supervision of a Probation Officer for a period of not less than 6 months nor more than 3 years. Any offence committed during this period renders him liable to punishment for the original offence.

The Conditions of a Probation Order must be explained and the Defendant must consent to the imposition of these conditions. The usual conditions are:

(a) To be of good behaviour and lead an industrious life.
(b) To notify the Probation Officer of any change of address.
(c) To keep in touch with the Probation Officer in accordance with instructions.

Exceptional conditions may be made as to residence and medical treatment.

**Community Service Order** – Any Offence for which a sentence of imprisonment can be given.

Community Service Orders are designed as an alternative to short custodial sentences. They provide a constructive disposal which has elements of punishment, reparation and rehabilitation. They are for offenders of either sex of 17-years and upwards who are convicted of an offence for which they could be sent to prison. The order requires the performance of between 40 and 240 hours of unpaid work during the offender's spare time. It should be completed within 12 months. Failure to comply results in breach proceedings when the Court may deal with the original offence or impose a fine of up to £50 and allow the order to continue.

**Money Payment Supervision Order**

A Money Payment Supervision Order may be made in respect of an offender who is required to pay a fine, costs, damages or compensation. A Court may appoint anyone it wishes to exercise supervision with a view to helping the offender meet his obligation to pay the sum ordered thereby avoiding imprisonment.

**Suspended Prison Sentence**

A court which passes sentence of imprisonment for a term of not more than two years may suspend the sentence for a specified period. The period for which a sentence may be suspended (the 'operational' period) is between one and three years. The result is that the sentence does not take effect unless, during the operational period, the offender commits another offence punishable with imprisonment when a court may then order the Suspended Sentence to take effect.

## Suspended Sentence Supervision Order
If the court believes that an offender is in need of help and guidance during the operational period of a suspended sentence, a Suspended Sentence Supervision Order may be made requiring a Probation Officer to supervise for the specified operational period.

## CUSTODIAL SENTENCES (ADULTS)

**Detention Centre** – Any offence which carries imprisonment (Male only).
A sentence for young men from 14 to 21 years providing a brisk regime calculated to impress upon them a sense of discipline and respect for authority. The minimum term possible is three months and the maximum six months. One third remission of sentence is normal. The sentence is followed by 12 months Supervision by a Probation Officer (or social worker if subject to a care order) under the terms of a Detention Centre Licence.

**Borstal Training** – Any offence which carries imprisonment.
Borstal Training is available for offenders aged between 15-21 years and the sentence is passed by the Crown Court only. The court makes such an order where, having regard to the circumstances of the offence, the offenders character and previous conduct, that he requires training for not less than six months. There is no such thing as remission, the discharge date is theoretically based on progress. Training is followed by Supervision for one year by a Probation Officer under the terms of a Borstal Licence.

## Imprisonment
For every offence the law indicates whether imprisonment may be imposed as a penalty and if so what the maximum term is. No person under 21 years may be sentenced to imprisonment unless the Court is satisfied that no other method of dealing with him is appropriate and has obtained a report for this purpose. The same considerations apply to a person who has attained the age of 21 and who has not previously been sentenced to imprisonment.

If the court does impose imprisonment it is bound to state its reason which will be entered in the warrant of commitment and in the Court Register.

The local Probation Office in a prisoner's home area will be notified of his imprisonment and a Probation Officer will be allocated to make contact during his sentence.

Prisoners (other than persons sentenced to Life Imprisonment) are eligible for release after serving two thirds of sentence subject to good conduct. Persons released otherwise than on licence need not accept any form of after-care or comply with any conditions, but they are offered voluntary after-care by Probation and After-Care Service.

Prisoners serving a determinate sentence of imprisonment are considered for parole ie. release on *parole licence,* after serving one third of their sentence or one year, which ever is the later. Parole may be granted if it is recommended by the Parole Board, parole licence remaining in force until the date on which the prisoner would have been released on remission if he had not been granted parole. A person on parole will normally be under the Supervision of a Probation Officer and is liable to recall either by the Home Secretary, if the Parole Board recommends or on revocation of his licence by a court.

Prisoners serving sentences of life imprisonment may be released on life licence subject to such conditions (ie, supervison by a Probation Officer) as the Home Secretary may specify. They remain liable for the rest of their lives to be recalled.

### SENTENCING OPTIONS (JUVENILES ONLY)

**Definitions and Presumptions**

**Child** – a person who has not attained the age of 14 years.

**Young Person** – a person who has attained the age of 14 years but has not attained the age of 17 years.
A child under the age of 10 years is conclusively presumed to be incapable of crime.
A child of 10 and under 14 years is presumed incapable of crime unless this is rebutted on proof of malice, ie, that he knew what he was doing was wrong.
Young Person 14-17 years – full criminal responsibility.

# SENTENCES IN CRIMINAL PROCEEDINGS

**Absolute Discharge** – as per adult.

**Conditional Discharge** – as per adult.

**Fine** – Child up to £50. Young Person up to £200 maximum.

## Supervision Order

Made to Local Authority or Probation Service. Maximum period of Supervision 3 years. It is the duty of the Supervising Officer to 'advise, assist and befriend'. Additional conditions may be inserted into the Supervision Order by the Court, eg, mental treatment, residence with a named individual, school attendance clause, intermediate treatment.

## Attendance Centre Order

Attendance Centres are designed to deal with young offenders whose future conduct may be expected to be influenced by the effect of deprivation of leisure time at the same time providing instruction in the constructive use of leisure and guidance in respect for the law and the property of others. Hours of attendance to be specified by the court – between 12-24 hours usually on Saturday afternoons.

**Detention Centre** – as per adult.
Where a juvenile is over 14 and the offence carries imprisonment. Maximum sentence of 3 months for those under 17 years.

**Borstal Training** – as per adult.

## Care Order

A Care Order authorises the committal of the juvenile to the care of the Local Authority, where the offence is punishable in the case of an adult, with imprisonment. The order lasts until the 18th birthday, but if the young person is already 16 years, until the 19th birthday.

## Hospital Order or Guardianship Order

## Recognizance

Binding over the parent in maximum of £50 for up to 3 years or until the juvenile is aged 18, to take proper care and exercise proper control over the juvenile.

## IMPRISONMENT OF YOUNG PERSONS

A person found guilty of murder when under the age of 18 years must be sentenced to detention During Her Majesty's Pleasure.

Where a person under 17 years is convicted on indictment of an offence for which an adult may be sentenced to imprisonment for 14 years or more, the court may sentence him to be detained in such place as the Home Secretary may direct.

Young Prisoners (under 21 years) sentenced to a term of more than one month are eligible for release on remission after serving 2/3rds of their sentence (as per adults) but unlike an adult a Young Prisoner serving imprisonment of less than 18 months is subject, after release, to Supervision by a Probation Officer for the following 12 months under the terms of a Young Prisoners Licence.

**Suspended Sentence and Suspended Sentence Supervision Order –**
as per adult.

# Appendix 4

## SOCIAL & ECONOMIC CONDITIONS OF ETHNIC MINORITIES IN WEST MIDLANDS COUNTY

### Distribution of Ethnic Minorities in West Midlands County

During the 1950s and 1960s the West Midlands conurbation was one of the biggest attractors of New Commonwealth migrants who largely replaced migrants from northern England, Scotland, Eire and Wales. By 1971 the conurbation contained over 10% (120,000) of the total New Commonwealth population in Great Britain, second only to London with over 41% (476,000). Figures below show the distribution of black residents within the West Midlands County:

### West Midlands County Council Household Survey 1976[1]
### Proportions of black residents:

| District | % |
|---|---|
| Birmingham | 12.3 |
| Coventry | 8.5 |
| Dudley | 2.7 |
| Sandwell | 7.9 |
| Solihull | 1.6 |
| Walsall | 6.1 |
| Wolverhampton | 14.9 |
| West Midlands County | 9.1 |

**Map 2** Divides the West Midlands County into 8 operational Probation Sub-Areas. Birmingham is divided into 4, Birmingham N.S.E. & W., forming the centre core, with Wolverhampton/Dudley-Warley/Walsall to the West and Coventry to the East.

---

[1]WMCC Structure Plan 'Social Conditions'.

**Map 3** Illustrates the geographical distribution of the ethnic minorities within these areas and shows the clear segregation of the black communities from the suburbs.

It is evident that Wolverhampton and Birmingham are the places with the greatest concentrations. In absolute numbers Birmingham (population 1,033,900) has the biggest black population and Dudley and Solihull have the smallest, as could be expected. However, it can be seen that *ALL* Probation Sub-Areas have a black population.

### Distribution of black population related to Social conditions

Areas within Districts with high concentrations of black people coincide with:

(a) the older privately rented housing accommodation (map 4)
(b) areas which suffer from bad physical and social conditions generally (map 5)
(c) areas with acute unemployment problems (map 6)

Whilst these factors contain the ingredients of the cycle of deprivation which can affect ALL who live in these areas, the West Midlands County Council point out that the black communities are highly represented in these areas and also face the additional problems of:

(d) prejudice and discrimination
> It is acknowledged in the West Midlands County Survey that prejudice and discrimination are problems affecting the majority of black people in the community, and are manifest in every facet of urban life and that the major reason for discrimination is skin colour. Care is advocated in policy making in order to 'avoid unconsciously assisting the more insidious manifestations of racism'[1]

(e) cultural differences
> Important cultural differences between ethnic groups including West Indians, Pakistanis, Indians and Bangladeshis are also taken into account at a local planning level, in order to meet cultural needs.

These findings in the West Midlands County Structure plans agree sub-

---

[1]WMCC Structure Plan 'Social Conditions'.

stantially with the situation outlined in 'Ethnic Minorities in the Inner City' – by Crispin Cross[2]

'Urban deprivation is defined as:

(1) incorporating physical characteristics which impair the quality of life of those who live in it and cannot escape from it.
(2) often marked by the relatively low provision of services and facilities to people who need them most by virtue of their economic poverty – reflecting the pressure of demand over the supply of resources.
(3) incorporating socially disadvantaged groups because such people are attracted to it in search of better living and other opportunities, and partly because such an environment incorporates groups of people who are victims of the cycle of deprivation (or transmitted deprivation).

The findings of this study point to the need for:

(a) priority to be given to ethnic minorities in social policies in the light of their greater need in general and in policies directed at alleviating some of the consequences of multiple deprivation in particular.
(b) modifications or adaptions in the ways in which social policies and specific programmes are presented to ethnic minority residents.
(c) the development of special programmes to meet the needs which are particular to ethnic minority groups and do not affect the indigenous population (eg, second language facilities).

West Midlands County also advocate 'initiatives to tackle the social, economic and housing issues which feed prejudice and conflict'.

Some opportunities already exist to assist such problem areas by affording them priority treatment in the allocation of resources. West Midlands Probation and After-Care Service has taken advantage of such resources through the Urban Aid Programme. (see 'Linked Projects' Section 4).

---

[2]CRE Publication.

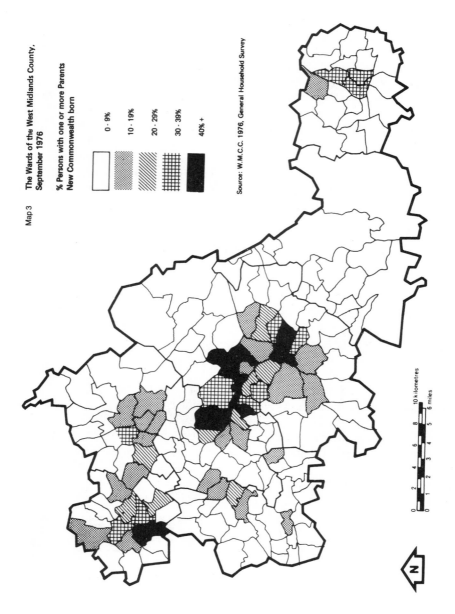

Map 3    The Wards of the West Midlands County,
          September 1976

% Persons with one or more Parents
New Commonwealth born

0 - 9%

10 - 19%

20 - 29%

30 - 39%

40% +

Source: W.M.C.C. 1976, General Household Survey

0   2   4   6   8   10 kilometres
0   1   2   3   4   5   6 miles

N

128

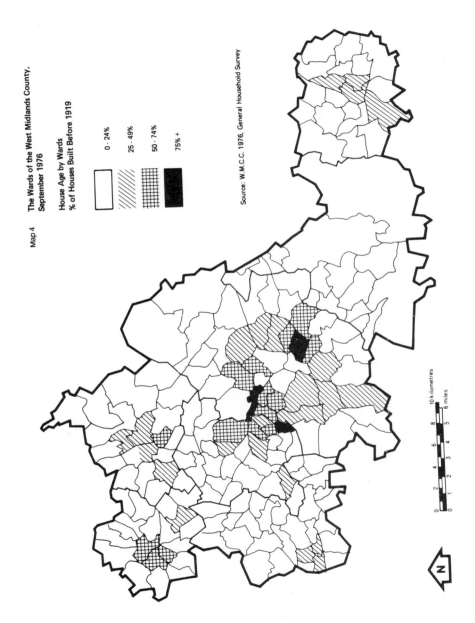

Map 4　**The Wards of the West Midlands County, September 1976**

**House Age by Wards**
**% of Houses Built Before 1919**

　0 - 24%

　25 - 49%

　50 - 74%

　75% +

Source: W.M.C.C. 1976, General Household Survey

10 kilometres

6 miles

0　1　2　3　4　5　6　8

N

129

Map 5 Environmental Priority Areas

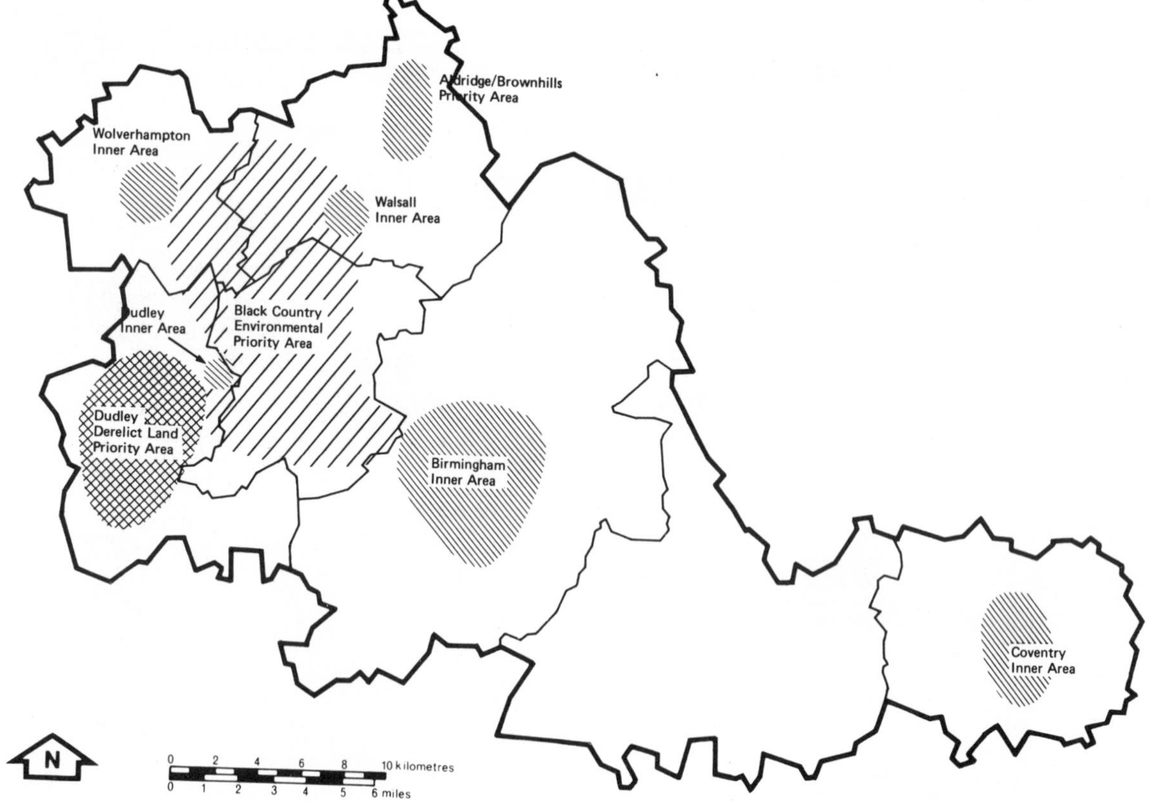
Aldridge/Brownhills
Priority Area
Wolverhampton
Inner Area
Walsall
Inner Area
udley
Inner Area
Black Country
Environmental
Priority Area
Dudley
Derelict Land
Priority Area
Birmingham
Inner Area
Coventry
Inner Area
N
0 2 4 6 8 10 kilometres
0 1 2 3 4 5 6 miles

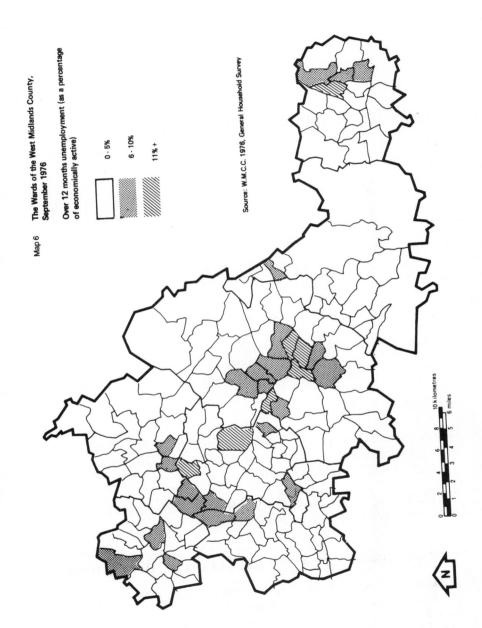

Map 6    **The Wards of the West Midlands County, September 1976**

**Over 12 months unemployment (as a percentage of economically active)**

0 - 5%

6 - 10%

11% +

Source: W.M.C.C. 1976, General Household Survey

N

10 kilometres

6 miles

0 1 2 3 4 5 6 8

# Appendix 5

## CLASSIFICATION OF ETHNIC GROUPS AND DEFINITIONS

Classification of ethnic groups used in the survey were agreed with Birmingham Community Relations Council as follows:

1. West Indian Origins

2. African Origins

3. Indian Origins

4. Pakistani Origins

5. Afro/Asians (ie, Kenyan or Ugandan Asians)

6. Mixed Racial Origins (specify)

7. Non British or Other Ethnic Origins (specify)

The term 'origins' refers to:

(a) Any person born in the country of ethnic origin.
(b) Any person born elsewhere (ie, Britain) with one or both parents born in the country of ethnic origin.

For the purpose of this survey Irish were not classified as a separate ethnic group and are therefore included in the 'white' group.

## 'ETHNIC MINORITIES' AND 'BLACK PEOPLE' – DEFINITIONS

'**Ethnicity** . . . is the sense of a particularly close relationship between people from the same place of origin'[1]

---

[1] Pears Encyclopaedia.

'It is suggested that when members of an ethnic group are in a privileged position (such as a host nation) they appeal to the sense of ethnicity to close ranks against outsiders, divisions based on ethnicity cutting across those based on social class. The less fortunate might be more likely to unite on a non-ethnic basis to improve their positions'.[2]

**'Ethnic Group** . . . is a group of people sharing a common heritage'.[3]

**'Ethnic Minority Groups** . . . are aggregates of people who are distinctive in race, religion, language or nationality from other members of the Society in which they live, and who think of themselves and who are thought of by others as being separate and distinct'.[4]

The use of terms such as 'Ethnic Minorities' and 'Ethnic Groups' cause confusion because they mean different things to different people. In this report quotations from the works of others include such terms and it is thought the intention is often to refer to black people.

The words **'black people'** are used in this report when specifically referring to persons of Afro/Asian/Caribbean descent irrespective of the country of birth, who consider themselves to be of such descent.

The words **'Ethnic Minorities'** or **'Ethnic Minority Groups'** are used to refer to cultural groups in a wider context.

---

[2]Pears Encyclopaedia.

[3]Encyclopaedia Britannica.

[4]Encyclopaedia Britannica.

# Appendix 6

## GLOSSARY OF ABBREVIATIONS

PACS            Probation and After-Care Service.

WMCPACS         West Midlands County Probation & After-Care Service.

CPO             Chief Probation Officer.

DCPO            Deputy Chief Probation Officer.

ACPO            Assistant Chief Probation Officer.

SPO             Senior Probation Officer.

SPO             Probation Officer.

CCETSW          Central Council for Education and Training in Social
                Work.

CRC             Community Relations Council.

CRE             Commission for Racial Equality.

CSO             Community Service Order.

CSU             Community Service Unit.

C & YP          Children and Young Persons.

CQSW            Certificate of Qualification in Social Work.

DC              Detention Centre.

EMLAG           Ethnic Minorities Liaison Advisory Group.

HAS             Handsworth Alternatives Scheme.

HO              Home Office.

MPSO            Money Payment Supervision Order.

NACRO           National Association for the Care and Resettlement
                of the Offender.

| | |
|---|---|
| SO | Supervision Order. |
| SSSO | Suspended Sentence Supervision Order. |
| SER | Social Enquiry Reports. |
| STEP | Special Temporary Employment Programme. |
| WMC | West Midlands County |
| WMCC | West Midlands County Council. |
| YOP | Youth Opportunities Programme. |

# SELECTED CRE PUBLICATIONS

**ETHNIC MINORITIES IN THE INNER CITY:** The Ethnic Dimension in Urban Deprivation in England — by Crispin Cross .......................................... £2.00

**FUND RAISING:** A Handbook for Minority Groups ............................... £1.50

**URBAN DEPRIVATION, RACIAL INEQUALITY AND SOCIAL POLICY:** A Report (HMSO)................................................................ £1.75

**ASPECTS OF MENTAL HEALTH IN A MULTI-CULTURAL SOCIETY** .............. 60p

**CARING FOR UNDER-FIVES IN A MULTI-RACIAL SOCIETY** .................... 60p

**FOSTERING BLACK CHILDREN** (Reprint) ...................................... 60p

**MULTI-RACIAL BRITAIN.** Social Services Response............................ £1.00

**WHO MINDS?:** A Study of Working Mothers and Childminding in Ethnic Minority Communities................................................................ 75p

**FIVE VIEWS OF MULTI-RACIAL BRITAIN:** Talks on Race Relations Broadcast by BBC TV ............................................................................ £1.00

**BETWEEN TWO CULTURES:** A Study in Relationship between Generations in the Asian Community in Britain — by Muhammad Anwar.................................... £1.00

**AS THEY SEE IT:** A Race Relations Study of Three Areas From a Black View-point — by Lionel Morrison............................................................. £1.25

**THE ELDERS IN ETHNIC MINORITIES:** Edited by Frank Glendenning .............. £1.00

**RACE RELATIONS IN BRITAIN:** A Register of Current Research................... 75p

**VOTES AND POLICIES:** Ethnic Minorities and the General Election, 1979 — by Muhammad Anwar .......................................................... 75p
£1.50

**BEYOND UNDERACHIEVEMENT:** Case Studies of English, West Indian and Asian School-Leavers at Sixteen Plus — by Dr Geoffrey Driver ........................ £1.00

**YOUTH IN MULTI-RACIAL SOCIETY:** The Urgent Need for New Policies ........... £1.50

**WHO'S DOING WHAT?** A Directory of Projects and Groups Involved in Race Relations. £1.00

**HALF A CHANCE?:** A Report on Job Discrimination Against Young Blacks in Nottingham £1.00

# PERIODICALS

**NEW COMMUNITY** — Three issues per annum. £2.50 per copy Annual Subscription:
(Index to volumes 1,2,3,4,5, & 6 at 50p each)  Individuals £6.00
Institutions £8.00

**NEW EQUALS** — Bi-monthly ............................................. Free

**EDUCATION JOURNAL** — Three issues per annum............................. Free

**EMPLOYMENT REPORT** — Quarterly ...................................... Free